Astrology
the
Supernatural
and the
Beyond

by

Sri Chinmoy

ASTROLOGY
the
SUPERNATURAL
and the
BEYOND

Sri Chinmoy

Copyright © Sri Chinmoy Centre
Third edition, 2018

Artwork: Jozef Klopacka
Author photo: Piyasi Morris

All rights reserved. No portion of this book may be reproduced without express written permission from the Publisher.

Reprinted with kind permission of Aum Publications,
New York.

ISBN 978-0-9957531-3-6

Blue Beyond Books Limited
4 Paget Road, Ipswich
IP1 3RP, United Kingdom

www.bluebeyondbooks.co.uk

Printed in Great Britain

Contents

ONE   Astrology and Prophecy   9

TWO   Spirituality, Psychic Power, Occult Power and Black Magic   25

THREE   The Spirit World   61

FOUR   Mediums and the Unseen World   93

FIVE   Man and the Universe   109

          Explanatory Notes   131

          About the Author   139

          Recomended Books by Sri Chinmoy   143

Editorial Note

Sri Chinmoy's words presented here have been selected from his writings, lectures and answers to questions, which he offered to spiritual seekers, university students and luminaries from all walks of life over the years. In the process of compiling this book — which included occasional excerpting text from longer passages — we have strived to stay true to the original context and convey Sri Chinmoy's philosophy as he expressed it during his life.

Foreword

*I*n the course of his numerous public meditations and university lectures around the world, Sri Chinmoy was asked thousands of questions on occultism, astrology, flying saucers, extraterrestrial beings and similar subjects. Normally, he was reluctant to discuss such things because he felt that satisfying a seeker's mental curiosity would not increase the person's aspiration or devotion to God. However, as a God-realised spiritual Master with free access to the different inner worlds, Sri Chinmoy was able to offer one of the few authoritative and definitive explanations of these phenomena, and from time to time he answered questions on these matters. This book presents some of the most interesting of these questions and Sri Chinmoy's answers.

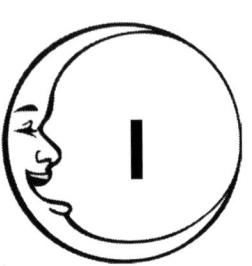

Astrology and Prophecy

Question: What do you think of astrology? Is there any truth to astrological predictions?

Sri Chinmoy: Astrology is a science. Even spiritual seekers call it an inner science, a spiritual science. Astrology is the song of the stars. That which has been decreed and that which has already entered into the world of manifestation is recorded in the stars. When astrology deals with the past, with what has already been recorded, it is nearly always correct. But astrology also lets us see potentiality, and it seeks to tell the future on the strength of the past. Expert astrologers are adept at entering into the truth of this realm. In most cases, when it is carefully and scientifically done, astrology is absolutely correct for ordinary people who have no faith in God or in themselves.

But if people have faith in themselves, with this faith they can transcend astrology. That is why we say that faith changes things by an unchanging will. If we have an unchanging will, fate can be changed. True, all our past deeds are recorded in the stars. But if we want to obliterate fate, it is like obliterating something on a tape recorder. I say something and it is recorded, but if I want to erase it, I can.

Astrology is one hundred per cent correct when one is totally in the physical world and is living an ordinary human life. When one enters into the inner life, the spiritual life, it is sixty or seventy per cent correct. If the aspirant is in touch consciously or unconsciously with his inner being, and if his inner being is constantly in touch with the Source, there will be many, many bad things that he can avoid. Finally, when one is consciously in communion with God, astrology does not function at all for that person, because everything in his life comes directly from God. True oneness with God is far beyond astrology. With our intense aspiration* if we say, "God, I don't want this," and if we are one with God, then God will say, "All right, then don't take it." Of course, this does not apply to beginners in

---

* See Explanatory Notes

the spiritual life. Only those who have an immediate inner communication with the Highest Being can go completely beyond the influence of the stars. But one does not remain a beginner always. In the course of time one becomes more and more advanced in the spiritual life, and more and more immune to the forces of one's past.

Now even if one is not a seeker, an astrological prediction may still be transcended. On a deeper level there is always a higher force called God's Grace. God's Grace can change anybody's fate. This Grace is almighty; it changes the occult possibilities and transcends the laws of astrology, which are God's cosmic Laws. Sometimes an astrologer's prediction is actually true, but it does not happen because of the divine grace. That is why astrology is only thirty-five or forty per cent correct when it deals with the future. When we know that there is something infinitely superior to astrological law, we should have faith in this. So my request to my disciples is not to have faith in horoscopes and palmistry. Have all faith in your aspiration. If you have total faith in your aspiration and in God's Grace, then your salvation will come. You need not worry about your future.

In India there are quite a few systems of casting horoscopes. The Bhrigu system is most significant. It was introduced thousands of years ago and now there are volumes upon volumes written about it, with everything recorded. You just give your chart to the brahmin, the astrologer who is dealing with this system, and he will turn the pages in front of you and tell you everything about your life. Very often it is true. Your life history has been written there. If the proper chart has been drawn, then he does not even have to cast a horoscope. It is already written there.

My eldest brother, who is an astrologer, went to an astrologer who was conversant with this system and who had all the old, sacred books where everything is written. When he showed my chart to this astrologer, the astrologer said that after the age of twelve, my horoscope would not function any more. He was absolutely correct, because at the age of thirteen I realised God and became immune to all the astrological laws.

One more incident I wish to tell you about the Bhrigu system. My maternal uncle went to an astrologer to have his horoscope cast according to this system. He and his wife did not have any children. In the horoscope it was mentioned that this couple would never have children because my uncle, who had been a hunter in his previous incarnation, had killed a deer which was pregnant. While the deer was breathing her last, her soul prayed to God, "O God, he has killed my baby inside me. Please do not give him any child in his next incarnation." God listened to the deer's prayer and in this incarnation my maternal uncle had no children. After my realisation I concentrated to see whether or not this story about my maternal uncle in his past incarnation was true, and I found that it was absolutely true.

Now this does not mean that everything astrologers say is true. Far from it. Last March a disciple of mine came to me crying that somebody had predicted her father would die that month. I said, "Well, if your father is meant to die, he will die according to the astrologer's prophecy." Then I concentrated and told her, "Don't worry. I am doing nothing. I am not bringing down God's Grace. I am not even praying to God for your father, but the prediction is wrong." Believe me, I did not pray to the Supreme in order to nullify the astrologer's prophecy, but her father is still sound and healthy. Another disciple's mother was supposed to die, according to astrologers, on the seventeenth or eighteenth of December. That disciple of mine cried bitterly. But I told him that this prediction was also wrong. His mother is still alive.

In India we know of many cases where astrology has failed, especially in situations involving a spiritual ashram. The astrologers may say that when a child is fourteen or fifteen his parents will die. But if, before the child reaches that age, his parents accept the spiritual life, they may live many years longer. Many Gurus have changed their disciples' fate. There are many stories about this in India. For example, an astrologer once said that someone was going to die on a certain day and at a particular time. But a spiritual figure told the man to come to him. The person came and the teacher placed him on the ground and covered him with mud, then sat there meditating. When the designated hour had passed, the Guru removed the mud covering his new disciple and said, "Now go to the astrologer and show him that you still exist on earth." There are many, many authentic cases like this one.

There are crises in our lives. Sometimes when we are young our lives are in danger. But if there is God's Grace, or if somebody such as our parents or relatives is consciously or unconsciously praying for us, then we can avoid the danger.

In horoscopes we see that many times death is written for a person. Astrologers mention that there will be danger and the person will die. But many of these people are still alive. Furthermore, we have lines in our palms that show how many years we shall live on earth. In some cases, anybody who knows palmistry will say that a person's life-line is only for, say, thirty-two or thirty-three years, but this person may be seventy-two or seventy-five years old now. Even among my disciples there are two or three women whose life-lines are completely broken. If a palmist reads their palms he would see just the two halves and be astonished that they are still on earth. How does it happen? Some higher power has been responsible. There is nothing that cannot be changed by the infinite Grace of the Supreme.

Question: What is your opinion about prophecy? Can the future really be known in advance?

Sri Chinmoy: When people make predictions, sometimes the predictions come true and sometimes they are simply wrong. Suppose your third eye* is open and you know that somebody is going to die tomorrow. If you tell him that he is going to die tomorrow, you are doing him the greatest harm because the fear that you are creating in him today will immediately take away all his life's joy, confidence and assurance. During his remaining hours, he will be dwelling already in the realm of death because of his fear. Even if your prediction does not come true, still the person is half-dead. What good does it do to tell him that he is going to die? This is not likely to have any good result.

Very often people make amazing predictions, positive predictions such as 'you will be favoured,' 'you will become a great person,' 'you will become something wonderful and the whole world will acclaim you.' When this kind of prediction is made we often see the malicious interference of the hostile forces. The person who has made the prediction has

---

* See Explanatory Notes

seen the truth, but his vision is not the vision of the Omnipotent; it is the vision of someone who has the capacity to see the truth, but not of the One who can create the truth, who can manifest the truth. When an ordinary person has the capacity to make predictions, he feels that he has created the truth; but that is not true. Only God has created the truth and only God has the power to nullify the truth or transform the truth. I personally do not like to predict anything, because very often we break the cosmic law in predicting the future. We do not allow this future to be expressed the way it was intended by God.

A disciple once went to his Master and said that an astrologer had predicted he would die that very day. The Master concentrated on the disciple and said, "Yes, it is destined, but I will bring down the Grace of the Almighty and I will be able to save you."

The disciple went back to the astrologer and told him, "My Master says your prediction won't come true."

The astrologer said, "I have made predictions hundreds of times and all my predictions have come true. If my prediction does not come true in your case, I will become your Master's disciple; and if my prediction comes true, then your Master will have to come and learn astrology from me."

The disciple told his Master what the astrologer had said, and the Master agreed to the bargain.

The day passed and nothing happened. So the astrologer went to the Master to become his disciple, and the Master explained to him, "Your prediction was absolutely true. Although there are people who make wrong predictions, your prediction was true. But I brought down the Grace of the Supreme for my disciple to counter his fate."

Question: Lately in newspapers and magazines I have been reading about prophecies that part of the world is going to be dissolved or sink into the ocean. Is there any truth in this?

Sri Chinmoy: The world is full of imagination. God has been very kind to us; He has given us imagination in infinite measure. Neither California nor Puerto Rico nor any part of the world is going to be dissolved. It is simply absurd and impossible, even if the astrologers say so. But this rumour creates great sensation. As for parts of the land sinking into the sea, well, there is always the possibility of this kind of change in the earth's surface, but it cannot be predicted with any accuracy by astrologers since there are always forces working which they cannot evaluate.

But why do we have to think of whether a particular place will last or not? Let us think of our own realisation. God-realisation* is our goal. To wonder whether this or that place will continue to exist will not help us in reaching our goal. If we can remain in God's Consciousness we are immortal, but if we remain in the earth-consciousness we will not be immortal. It is the divinised consciousness that makes us immortal, and not the place where we live.

Question: Peter Hurkos**, who is well-known now throughout the world, was an ordinary person before he fell off a ladder near his house and struck his head. When he regained consciousness, he was able to look into the future and tell what would happen. He helps the police discover murderers and all kinds of things. What do you think happened when he fell down and hit his head?

---
* See Explanatory Notes
** See Explanatory Notes

Sri Chinmoy: The thing is that we have to know something about his past. In this life he was an ordinary person, but in his past incarnations probably he had already developed this power. At a particular hour this man got a shock and immediately he revived his old life and the power he had from his past incarnations.

Many, many times this happens to the most ordinary people: to servants and menial workers. When they are attacked with serious diseases, they get all kinds of spiritual power; all their past powers are revealed. The disease is the last stroke. We call it the stroke of inner purification. The stroke serves as the inner purification of their being, of their life. It is not an accidental stroke; it is just an occasion used by these powers to come to the fore again.

Question: What is the difference between astrology and Yoga?

Sri Chinmoy: Astrology does not have the power to change our fate, but spirituality or Yoga* does have this power. The difference between astrology and Yoga is that astrology only indicates; it indicates the future on the basis of the past, but it does not

---
* See Explanatory Notes

change it. Yoga, however, can actually defeat the past and shape the future. Astrology plays its role most effectively until one has entered into deeper spirituality. There astrology bows down, as you bow down to me. Before one accepts spirituality, astrology is very powerful, like a lion. Then when one enters into a deeper spiritual life, astrology becomes a tiny household cat.

Question: Once you said that you tried to help three disciples whom you saw were destined to die. You said that with two of them you succeeded, and the third you weren't sure of at the time. What does it all depend on? The person's receptivity?

Sri Chinmoy: Mostly receptivity. I am ready to give. If they can receive, they will be all right; otherwise, they will not. Sometimes they resist, or do not have any life-energy. If there is even an iota of life-energy, if the doctor gives an injection, then perhaps the person may revive. At least there is some possibility and hope. But if the person is absolutely dead, what good will an injection do? Similarly, no matter how much power you bring down from above, the case is absolutely hopeless if the person's life-energy is too limited.

Question: Is there any significance if a child is born during an eclipse of the sun or the moon?

Sri Chinmoy: An astronomer or an astrologer would be in a better position than I to answer this question. From the spiritual point of view, I wish to say that a child born during an eclipse of the sun brings into the world tremendous energy. If this energy is not channelled through spiritual paths early in the child's life, it can cause a lot of trouble. The child can become unruly and undisciplined and can use this energy for a destructive purpose. If the child is spiritually developed, he can use his boundless energy to climb the heights of spirituality and do the work of God in the world. Then again, if such a child is not spiritually inclined, still his energy may become perfectly balanced through the Grace of God. Then he can also do constructive work in the world.

A child born during a lunar eclipse has a sweet, poised disposition. If he is spiritually inclined he will reach his goal through his sweet and poised personality and his love for the Divine. If the person is not spiritual, there may be a tendency toward sloth and drowsiness, and he may spend his time aloof from everything and inwardly sleeping.

Question: The stars affect us, the earth affects us and so on. Now when we meditate, do we affect any other planets, for instance, or anything else?

Sri Chinmoy: It depends on who is meditating. If someone is an aspirant of the highest rank and if his meditation is bearing fruit, solid fruit, at that time it does affect the planets. It enters into the planets and creates new life. From the world atmosphere it brings a kind of subtle spiritual energy into the planets. But if a spiritual Master meditates, his meditation can enter into any planet anywhere in God's universe, if he wants. A highly advanced seeker who is on the verge of realisation can also affect the planets. When these people meditate, they can enter into the planets, or they can offer the result of their meditation to the planets. That is being done almost every day.

Spirituality, Psychic Power, Occult Power and Black Magic

Question: What is occultism, and on what plane do the occult forces exist?

Sri Chinmoy: Occultism is a science. Occultism is pure when it is practised in the subtle physical or in the supra-physical planes. Some people call this the astral plane while others call it the vital world. But it is actually in the inner vital* that we can see the source of occultism. The occult forces are the forces of our hidden nature. The occult world is the subtle physical, and the vital and supra-physical.

If you consciously and deliberately enter into the vital plane, the first thing that happens is that you are caught by the vital beings. These beings will very often gladly give you some of their occult power

---

*   See Explanatory Notes

to use. For some time, they will allow you to make use of their own occult power and then they will try to control you. These beings have countless silly desires, which they try to fulfil through the seeker whom they have entrusted with their occult forces.

If a seeker is true and genuine, and if he enters into the vital planes for spiritual purposes while widening his inner consciousness, there is no danger. This is because the seeker is firm in his aspiration. He wants only the spiritual expansion of his inner and outer nature and does not care for the so-called occult forces. But the seeker who has tampered with the occult world sees that his goal is a far cry and, at the same time, finds that he has been mercilessly captured by the beings in the vital planes. There he is lost, totally lost. There are many, many seekers who started their spiritual journey with all sincerity, but who were caught on their way by the occult forces and could not reach their goal.

Question: There have been many books written about the occult. Do you feel that they are of any real value?

Sri Chinmoy: I am fully aware that many of you are studying books that deal with occultism, but my sincere request to you is that you do not study books on occultism unless they were written by spiritual Masters or realised souls. Most of the books on occultism are collections of fanciful ideas. By merely studying books on occultism, one can never get even an iota of occult power. Books can teach the secrets of occultism, but one can only develop the powers by going deep within and enlarging one's consciousness, or by sincerely crying to bring these hidden forces to the fore, hopefully for the sake of the Divine only.

Question: Can you tell me the difference between spiritual power and occult power?

Sri Chinmoy: Spiritual power is very vast and luminous. It is constantly expanding both the finite and the infinite. If something is little, the spiritual life will make it bigger. If it is already very big, spirituality will make it bigger still. Occult power is of a different kind. You can say it is a direct, pointed, immediate power – very sharp, like the edge of a sword.

When spiritual power is used, it is all peace, all harmony. If somebody is applying spiritual power to you, you will feel that there is dynamic power, but at the same time there is no aggression in it. It is like seeing the sea when it is calm and quiet. When it is turbulent with waves, you are frightened. But when the sea is in silence, at that time you are not afraid. In both cases, however, the same power is there. When you enter into the consciousness of the sea, you see that it has tremendous, boundless power. Spiritual power is a quiet, infinite expanse, like a calm sea with no aggressive motion in it. But it has solid power, dynamic solid strength.

In occult power, on the other hand, there is a kind of movement which is almost always restless. A child has strength; an adult also has strength. A child's power is always revealing or manifesting; the child is constantly wanting to express this power. But a grown-up person knows that he has power and can use it at his command, so he does not feel the need to express it constantly. A possessor of occult power rarely has peace, whereas the possessor of spiritual power is inundated with peace. A possessor of occult power makes a tremendous outer show of his occultism; a Yogi with spiritual power tries inwardly to change the face of the world.

Occult power is used in a negative way very often. In occultism you will see that the power is practically like that of a ferocious animal. When unwise people use occult power, it is only for destruction. It can be positive only if it is guided by a spiritual Master. Possessing occult power is like walking on a rope – very dangerous and risky. Having spiritual power is like walking along a solid road, where there is no danger. And if one has both spiritual power and occult power, then, too, there is no difficulty or danger. With spiritual power we will be able to succeed – slowly, steadily and unfalteringly. Infallibly we will be able to do what we set out to do. With occult power, if we use it correctly, we may do what we want to do immediately and directly. If this tremendous speed of occultism feels the necessity of surrendering to the wisdom-light of spiritual power, then occultism is a veritable blessing for humanity. It is a veritable boon from God, for humanity has no patience; it wants to get everything done sooner than at once. But if occultism stands against spiritual power, then it is negating truth itself. And when it negates truth, it is creating destruction in humanity and for humanity.

If one wants to practise occultism in order to awaken the consciousness of humanity, then he first has to conquer fear: physical, vital, mental and psychic fear. If occultism is to be practised to serve the Supreme, the divinity in humanity, one has to conquer the lower vital, which we will call sex. This impure, unlit urge in our human nature must be totally conquered. Then if one can have the realisation that one is living the Eternal Life in the fleeting life, the infinity, eternity and immortality that he has achieved in his own inner being or consciousness can be used to serve humanity in a divine way. At that time, occult power will be a real blessing.

I wish my dedicated disciples who are interested in occult power to bear this in mind: first spirituality and then occultism; first divinity and then humanity. When one knows divinity and can remain in divinity, only then can one serve humanity. Manifestation without realisation is no manifestation at all. It is like a body without life. Once I reach the goal and become the goal, then everything is inside me. Nothing can disturb me; nothing can destroy me; nothing can harm me in any way. Everything in God's creation can be seen, felt and accepted. The realised person is in a position to handle both spiritual power and occult power. After realising the truth, while manifesting it on earth, one has to take help from all planes, including the occult.

Spirituality is far superior to occultism. The occult region and occult practice are also part of God's creation. But we do not have to go through the occult regions if what we want is God-realisation. If one wants God and God alone, then I must say that occultism cannot help even an iota in one's God-realisation. But spirituality is absolutely necessary to realise God.

A real spiritual aspirant does not care for occultism at all. But on his way toward the Highest, occult power sometimes automatically comes to him as a test, to see whether he is going to be impressed by it and show the world his capacity to perform miracles or whether he is going to use it properly and divinely. Sometimes, when an aspirant is on the verge of realisation, the occult powers from various planes of consciousness come and touch his feet. They say, "Master, use us. We will be at your service; we will make no mischief. Only use us for the fulfilment of your realisation." In the case of quite a few spiritual Masters this has happened. And your Master is one of them.

I have used occult power many, many times, but only when I have been asked to by the Supreme in me. And I use it only to help inwardly. Outwardly I am reluctant to use my occult power because I will be misunderstood. And never will I use it to punish or torture anyone. Occult power is very dynamic, but often people do not take dynamism from it. They take aggression from it instead and use this aggressive power to harm others or to attain their personal desires.

Occult power is not bad in itself. Some people say that when a person gets occult power he will misguide others and ruin himself. In India some spiritual figures do not care for occult power at all. But this power itself is not bad; rather, it is how you use it. If you have fire, you can burn yourself, or you can cook food. If you have a knife, you can use it to stab someone or you can use it to carve a beautiful statue. To some extent it is true that if you don't have a knife, then of course you cannot do anything bad. But there are many good things which you may not be able to do, either. It is we who must use occult power wisely if and when we get it.

Some spiritual Masters in India advise their students not to deal at all with the occult forces, but to practise the spiritual life first. Then one will attain spiritual power, which can never create problems. This is what they say. By nature, spiritual power does not have that aggressive or destructive quality which occult power has, but even spiritual power can be misused, if one does not listen to the dictates of his inner being or to the Supreme.

There are also spiritual aspirants who practise spirituality and occultism together. They say that during the day you should practise spirituality and during the night you should practise occultism. Let spirituality and occultism walk side by side. This path is a bit dangerous. Many have tried, and most of them have failed to combine the two properly. The safest and most effective way is to launch into the spiritual path and widen one's own consciousness into infinity and eternity. At that time you will have full mastery in the occult world.

If a spiritual Master has the capacity to use spiritual power, you may ask whether he is able to use occult power as well, without making any mistakes. The answer is no. When a spiritual Master uses spiritual power, usually he uses it well. But when it comes to occult power, he does not actually misuse it; rather, he simply may not know how to handle it. There is a tremendous conflict between spiritual power and occult power when the Master is not of the highest calibre. If this happens what should he do? He should totally discard his occult power. He should say, "I don't want it. It is too dangerous. Let me use only spiritual power which is an infinite sea of light and bliss. This light and bliss is power enough for me."

If you practise Kundalini Yoga even a very little – say only fifteen minutes a day – along with your real aspiration and meditation, you will see that your psychic or occult centres are being opened. But if you enter into the inner life just to get occult power so you can show the world your capacity, then real spirituality will never dawn in your life. If you want to open your heart centre and show miracles so people will appreciate and admire you, and if you think that you will get more inspiration from their appreciation and admiration, I must say here that you are making a mistake. In other cases, when you do something and are extolled to the skies, you may get more inspiration to do it better. But in this case it is not like that. If you display some of your occult power and others appreciate you, you can rest assured that this is your downfall. You will not be inspired; on the contrary, instead of going deep within to get the real realisation, you will go on increasing your occult power. Occult power is all temptation.

The more you display occult power, the quicker you will lose it, because you have not been able to become one with the source. The source of occult power is light – quite limited, but still most pure light. Therefore, I always say that if you are going to deal with light, then you should deal with spiritual light. If it is limited, no harm, for it will not cause any danger. You may get a headache if you invoke too much, but it will not destroy you. Even if you bring down spiritual power beyond your capacity, it will not totally destroy you. But if you draw occult power into your system beyond your capacity, you will end up in a mental asylum. It is that dangerous, that destructive.

Our first wish should be to please the Supreme. In order to please Him, we have to give Him all our aspiration, and lay everything at His Feet. Once we have pleased Him, it is up to Him whether He will give us spiritual power or occult power, or both. If He wants to give us spiritual power, well and good. If He wants to give us occult power, well and good. If we have surrendered to His Will and He gives us occult power, rest assured that He will also give us the capacity to use it properly for Him.

If you want to please the Supreme in your own way, you will do many insincere things to please Him. You will try to please Him by hook or by crook. You will even go to the length of trying to flatter or bribe Him if your nature is not pure. But if your nature is pure, absolutely pure, snow-white, then you will try to please Him the way He wants to be pleased. If you can do that, if you can please God in His own way, all occult power, all spiritual power will be at your feet, serving you.

What the world needs is to please God. By pleasing Him, it will become ready for illumination. But the world is doomed to disappointment because it cries for power. If the world wanted God's Love, then by this time the world would have been saved, illumined, perfected and immortalised.

Question: Can you please explain what psychic power is and in what way it differs from spiritual power?

Sri Chinmoy: Psychic power is usually the power which a child has on the strength of his complete and constant oneness with his parents. He claims the inner possessions of his parents as his very own. Needless to say, this claim is well-founded. The parents, too, get tremendous joy in seeing and observing that their child entirely depends on them for his revelation and manifestation. Psychic powers are not indomitable. They can be and often are attacked by undivine forces. But the Supreme always takes the side of the psychic being which embodies the psychic power, and saves the psychic being.

Of course, the psychic being with its psychic power eventually can grow into a most powerful and most fulfilling being. Since the psychic being evolves, the gradual increase of psychic power is not only possible, but also inevitable. The manifestation of psychic power is a subtle, delicate, soft and lucid way of the divine manifestation in fairly advanced seekers.

With psychic power an individual can perform miracles. With this power one acquires the capacity to identify oneself with, and thereby see, the present, past and future of others, as well as one's own. Although it is a manifestation of divine power, psychic power has tremendous beauty, like the beauty of a flower or the beauty of the moon. This psychic beauty, in itself, is a tangible power.

Roughly speaking, psychic power is the power of a child, although this power can become boundless through its most intimate oneness with the Source. Spiritual power is the power of a grown man, although he may not use it wisely all the time. Occult power is the power of a restless or dynamic youth. Spiritual power is the power of a calm and quiet sea. Occult power is the power of a sudden mighty wave. Spiritual power is usually not as swift as occult power. But occult power very often breaks instead of building. Spiritual power always gives importance to building the Palace of Truth, slowly, steadily, unerringly and convincingly.

Whatever spiritual power does is sound, solid and lasting. Spiritual power has confidence from within and assurance from above. For the total manifestation of divinity on earth, all the psychic powers and all the occult powers must follow the lead of the spiritual power in order to reach the Absolute Supreme.

Question: I have been told that I am in the process of developing psychic powers. Should I continue visiting spiritualistic centres with this point in mind?

Sri Chinmoy: In your case, I wish to tell you frankly that it would be unwise to develop these psychic faculties right now. Why? Because I can see in your eyes that you are a very sincere person. You should not be satisfied with these psychic powers. Your soul wants to go far, farther, farthest. There are people who do not have the aspiration to go to the Highest, the Ultimate. They are satisfied with little bits of psychic power and do not want to go further. I might advise some people to develop their psychic faculties. But in your case, if you develop these faculties they will stand in your way, and you will not be able to go further and achieve the ultimate in your life. Now it is you who have to make a choice: whether you want to be satisfied with a piece of candy or you want to wait for the infinite truth, the infinite treasure of the Almighty.

If you are endowed with some psychic faculties, you will only try to use these faculties, and you will become enamoured of them. Very often people who get a little bit of psychic capacity, psychic power, become satisfied, and then they try to apply it to this person and that person, in season and out of season. It is like a child who has some fascinating toys and plays with them all the time. He will neglect his studies and remain a fool. If the child is sincere or earnest and gives value to his studies, then he will stop playing and start studying, because he knows that he has to study to become a man of wisdom.

Another danger with these psychic faculties is that they are very often threatened by the spirits. Those who develop the psychic faculties may not be spiritually or occultly strong. The psychic faculties come from the psychic world. They are very subtle, soft, or you can say, delicate. Very often they are threatened by occult powers which are sometimes very fierce, dynamic, arrogant and destructive. The hungry unsatisfied spirits will try to enter into the psychic faculties of the aspirant and take away all the aspiration that he had before he paused in his spiritual journey to develop his psychic powers. But if one makes true spiritual progress, inner progress, without caring for the psychic capacities, one will undoubtedly have all these faculties at the end of his journey, after he has realised God.

You will never be the loser if you do not pay any attention to this psychic capacity, because it will be developed in you automatically when all your centres are opened during your deep meditation. To achieve this meditation, you have to go to a God-realised spiritual Master who can teach you individually and who can also protect you from the attack of the wrong forces.

Right now, to be frank with you, there are already four forces that are constantly attacking you. Please be very careful about these forces. These four forces are already hovering around you. They are not good; they are undivine forces. On the one hand, your psychic faculties are being opened, or are about to open; on the other hand, there are forces, negative forces, which are trying to destroy you. So please go deep within. Cry inwardly for God's Protection and for God's Illumination, and these four forces will leave you. They are bound to leave you.

Question: Are psychic powers of benefit, or are they in a way a hindrance to self-realisation?

Sri Chinmoy: Psychic power does not help us in any way to realise God. But psychic power can be used, should be used and must be used if it is the Will of the Divine, after God has given us self-realisation. One of the great Indian spiritual Masters, Sri Ramakrishna*, used to say that to acquire psychic power is to destroy the possibility of self-realisation. You will attain your psychic power, but God will be denied to you, he would say.

Who is the possessor of all powers? God. When we become one with the Possessor, all His possessions immediately become ours. But without caring for the Possessor, if we cry for the possession, its attainment will hinder us on our journey to the ultimate goal. It is really a blessing not to have the psychic powers before major realisation. If we get them too soon, we shall be all the time in the world of showing off, in the world of miracles, in the

---
* See Explanatory Notes

world of magic, and not in the world of aspiration, dedication and realisation.

Ramakrishna's greatest disciple, Swami Vivekananda* – originally called Naren – was once asked by his Master, "Naren, I have practised austerities for many years; now look at me – I have all these high siddhis. Would you like to have them from me? You do not have to meditate because I have done it for you. I will give you all my powers." Naren's immediate answer was, "Will they help me in my Self-realisation?" The Master replied, "My dear Naren, no. No, they won't. For Self-realisation the psychic powers don't count. But if you want to, you can use them after Self-realisation. And if you have these psychic powers, naturally people will flock to you, and you will be better able to serve God in humanity." The disciple said, "No, thank you. Let me realise God first. Then I shall think of attaining these psychic powers." Then Ramakrishna, in front of his other disciples, blessed his dearest disciple most profoundly and said, "I knew it. It is you who can pass my test. Had I asked the same question of anybody else, like a greedy person he would have said, 'Yes, yes, please give me the

---

* See Explanatory Notes

powers. It is so kind of you.' But I knew your heart is absolutely pure. You want God, God alone."

Question: The fakirs in India who have these powers, do they devote them to the good principles of Yoga or do they use them for business?

Sri Chinmoy: Actually, many have deviated from the path of truth. For those who have done this, their psychic power is just like black magic. It does not serve any spiritual purpose. If somebody is sick and God tells you that He wants you to cure that particular person, or if somebody is in imminent danger and God wants you to save that person, you should use your psychic powers. But psychic power should be used only when it is requested or approved by God. Most people who are using these powers in India and other places are not using them in accordance with God's Will. They are just satisfying their own pride, vanity and ego. They are going against the Law of God. But they are making a terrible mistake, and their punishment will be very serious in their next life.

Question: *Is it true that psychic powers do not develop or manifest spontaneously in Yogis, but have to be developed through exercises or other means?*

Sri Chinmoy: There are seven major psychic centres in our body. These centres are not in the physical, but in the subtle body. At the crown of the head is one called Sahasrara, the thousand-petalled lotus. Between the eyebrows, a little above, is the place of vision called Ajna chakra. At the base of the throat is the chakra for speech and externalisation; we call it Vishuddha. And in the centre of the chest we have Anahata, the heart chakra. Many people get their psychic power mostly from here. At the navel we have Manipura. At the spleen there is another centre, Svadhisthana. And below, at the base of the spine, we have one chakra called Muladhara. Muladhara, Svadhisthana, Manipura, Anahata, Vishuddha, Ajna and Sahasrara: these are the seven chakras.

When a seeker consciously or unconsciously concentrates on these psychic centres, he develops psychic power. He may not know the actual name of the centre, but if he concentrates on the correct spot, automatically he acquires some intuitive power. To get the chakras to open and the Kundalini to start functioning, you have to concentrate on each chakra. That is one way to get psychic power – by means of spiritual discipline. Especially in the West, I hear many people saying that he has psychic power or she has psychic power, even though the person may not have even an iota of psychic power. Some people get a little intuitive feeling from the plane of intuition or from the physical mind, where there is subtle intuition, and they claim that they have psychic power. But it is not so easy to have psychic power. One has to work hard in order to attain it.

At the same time, if a Guru* or spiritual Master wants to, he can infuse that power into you without your having to meditate or practise Kundalini Yoga. It is a spiritual Master's privilege to give these powers, but it all depends on God's Will. If God wants to give you psychic power, during your sleep you will get a kind of mantra which is meant for you. At that time the figure or being appearing in your dream will tell you how many thousands of times you have to repeat that particular mantra. It will not be necessary to concentrate on a particular

---

* See Explanatory Notes

centre. You just have to repeat that mantra a certain number of times and then you will get psychic power. This even happens in the case of realisation. Most people realise God by practising spirituality throughout their life, but there are some who need not practise the spiritual life at all. In a dream God enters into the person and illumines his consciousness, and anyone with spiritual vision will see that he is liberated and realised.

It is not always necessary to cry consciously for psychic power either. When one becomes a Yogi, his centres often open spontaneously, and psychic power automatically comes. Even if one does not care for psychic power, it usually comes when one is advancing fast, very fast, towards his goal. If occult power comes as a blessing and does not prevent one from manifesting his inner divinity, then there is no harm in it. But if it stands in one's way as a curse or an obstacle, if it tempts the person and causes him to lose his speed or be diverted from his path, then he has to reject it bravely and concentrate on reaching his goal first.

Question: Would you call the ability to communicate directly with one's own Master without the use of the spoken word a form of psychic power?

Sri Chinmoy: Psychic power is not required to contact one's own Master. It is done through devotion, through implicit faith. Where is the Master? You are here in Puerto Rico and your Master perhaps is in New York, you say. But no! He is deep inside your heart, deep in the inmost recesses of your heart. If you want to contact your Master at any time, just enter into and plumb the depths of your heart, and you will find him there.

Psychic power is not required, but only devotion and faith. When you have devotion, the Master, or the person whom you are praying to, is at your beck and call. Sri Krishna, India's foremost spiritual Master, said, "It is easy for God to give power, light, bliss and all other divine qualities to a disciple. But if He gives devotion to the disciple, which is also a divine blessing, then He is caught. The moment the disciple gets devotion, the disciple can rest assured that his Master has become his perfect slave. A true devotee is very, very rare in this world. But a man of knowledge and wisdom, a man of light or a man of peace can very often be found."

Lord Krishna had a very intimate disciple named Vidhura, who was very, very poor. It happened that one day Lord Krishna visited Vidhura's house. Vidhura could not give him rice or a proper meal, so he served Sri Krishna a very simple meal on plantain leaves. Sri Krishna's heart swam in a sea of ecstasy and delight. What did he do? First he ate the meal, then he ate the whole plantain leaf. Vidhura asked, "Master, what are you doing? You are eating the plantain leaf. This is not food!" Sri Krishna said, "O Vidhura! How can I separate your food from the plantain leaf? How can I separate your devotion from your existence? In your meal I see devotion, in your body I see devotion, in your heart I see devotion, in your plantain I see devotion. Whatever I see with you, around you and in you is all devotion. I can no more separate the meal from the leaf than I can separate your soul from your body." So, this is what happens when one has true devotion for God, for the Supreme. One gets the Supreme by his side all the time.

Now I wish to say something about faith. I am sure that all of you have heard about the Ganges, India's most sanctified river. It is said that whoever takes a dip in the Ganges will be freed from all sins. Throughout the year you can commit all kinds of sins, and then if you just enter into the river, all these sins will disappear. This is our Indian belief. How stupid we are only God knows. Once Parvati, the consort of Lord Shiva, asked Lord Shiva, "Is it true that if once a man takes a dip in the Ganges all his sins will vanish in the twinkling of an eye? Do people have such faith?" He said to his consort, "Well, the best thing is for me to demonstrate it. Look, both of us will take human form and sit on the bank of the Ganges. I will be a very old man and you will be an old woman. You will be holding a baby in your lap and I will take away the life from the baby. Then immediately you start shedding bitter tears and crying that we have lost our only child. Many will come to console you and you will tell them: 'If my son is blessed by a person who feels that he has no sin, he will come back to life.'"

They took human form and sat on the banks of the Ganges. Hundreds had come to swim and bathe in the river. Parvati said, "All of you here know that the moment you enter into the Ganges, all your sins will no longer exist. Go and have a dip and then bless my child, and he will come back to life." Hundreds of persons passed by, but nobody wanted to do it. They were ready to swim, they were ready to take a dip or bathe in the Ganges for hours, but they knew that it would have no effect on the child. They would touch the child, but he would not come back to life. This went on for hours. Finally, the bystanders saw a middle-aged man approach the lady who had lost her only child. This man had just come out from a bar. He smelled very unpleasant and, according to Indian standards, was what you would call 'characterless.' The man came to her and asked, "Why are you crying?" She said, "I am crying because nobody is coming to bless my child, although everybody here knows that the moment they bathe in the Ganges all their sins will leave and they will be able to bring my child back to life."

"You are crying for that? I have faith. Let me go." He jumped into the Ganges, and in a couple of minutes he came back and touched the child. Immediately the child returned to life. Then Lord Shiva said, "See! Out of thousands only one person had faith in the Ganges!" And with this Lord Shiva, Parvati and the child disappeared.

Whenever we do anything we say that we have faith, but we are only fooling ourselves. This man never cared for the spiritual life or anything, but he knew that the Ganges actually came from the Himalayas. All India's spiritual Masters have great admiration for the Himalayas, and most of the Indian Vedic Seers meditated in the caves of the Himalayas. This man had boundless faith in the Ganges. Most of us would have gone to the Ganges but would not have dared to touch the child, because nobody wants to be a laughing stock. When it comes to the practical life, most of us will fail. And almost all of us who might have come and touched the child would have seen that we were not successful, because we lacked true faith in the Ganges. But that particular man did have faith in the Ganges. If we have true faith in God, we need not meditate twenty-four hours a day; just a few minutes will serve the purpose. If we have that soulful faith in God, then God takes care of us.

Question: Is it possible that some people are practising negative occultism without realising it, just by malicious talking or other things?

Sri Chinmoy: Any force, positive or negative, immediately creates a world of its own. Each time we release an idea, we are creating a world of our own. But if we say that just by using negative thoughts we are practising occultism, it would be absolutely wrong. Similarly, by using positive thoughts, we are not creating a higher spiritual life.

Negation and destruction are almost always in the unsatisfied vital world where we very often practise occultism. Positive assertion and one-pointed will to reveal and manifest one's divinity is always done in the inner world or the psychic world. We have to know how we are using these powers and why we are using them.

Question: Are we losing anything by not developing ourselves in the occult world?

Sri Chinmoy: We do not lose anything, for it is the spiritual world that will give us our highest realisation. If we live in the inner world, the spiritual world, then automatically we get the invaluable wealth of the spiritual world. And we will see that the occult forces and all the other forces are housed there. We do not lose anything by not concentrating on the occult world.

Question: I thought occultism was something like black magic. Can you explain what it is?

Sri Chinmoy: Yes. Occultism in the lowest sense is black magic. Occultism in the purest sense is the dynamic aspect of the Divine Force, the Universal Force. When occultism is practised to destroy God's universal harmony, it is called black magic. This black magic that we see in the East and the West is absolutely perverted occultism. Black magic deals very often with the impurity and darkness of our nature. Pure occultism, true occultism, has nothing to do with black magic or black magicians.

I know of a woman in Miami who used black magic to make her sister give birth to a stillborn child. The woman did not have the power herself, so she went to a black magician in Haiti who used his power. He created all kinds of problems, just by using occult power from Haiti. The sister suffered from many ailments which the doctors could not cure. She will have to go all the way to Haiti to beg this stupid black magician to help her out of the difficulties created for her by her own sister.

In Manhattan we had two or three cases of this kind of black magic. A disciple's sister went to Haiti. Afterwards, her husband could not walk, dishes full of food dropped while he was holding them and many other things happened – all from occult power. The husband came to the Indian Consulate to meditate with me. He even came once or twice to see me at my house. He was cured, and then he left.

In the occult world, ordinary occultists fight like cats and dogs. Worse, in fact, for at least cats and dogs get tired. Ordinary occultists meditate, get a little power, and then, instead of following the right, spiritual path, they use their power to try to steal the power of other occultists.

A black magician can never harm a spiritual person who is realised or has spiritual power. A realised spiritual person, however, has the power to threaten the occultists and the black magicians, but he usually will not do it. When a spiritual person uses occultism, he uses it in a divine way. If there is a serious attack and somebody is going to fall from the spiritual path or is going to have a serious accident in his inner or outer life, I shall immediately use occult power if the Divine at that time wants me to be the instrument to help that particular person. This is pure occult power.

In India, black magicians have tried many times to punish spiritual Masters or destroy their spiritual power. The result was that they had to surrender all their black magic powers to the spiritual Masters. Many times occultists have tried to steal the powers of spiritual Masters who were sleeping. The Masters rest for only two or three hours, sometimes not even taking any sleep. When they lose consciousness, they do not keep any connection with the physical. At that time, an occultist can enter into the spiritual Master and try to take away his spiritual power. But these occultists are fools because spiritual Masters are always guided and protected by the Omniscient and the Omnipotent. The occultists will lose and have to surrender all their occult powers to the spiritual Masters. Then the occultists cry and cry. Some of these former occultists are now disciples of the spiritual Masters who have taken away their powers. Some black magicians who came to torture spiritual Masters lost their undivine, evil tendencies and became white magicians. They went to a person who was all compassion; and they were saved.

At the end of 1963, a very well-known Indian Muslim occultist from Hyderabad came to Pondicherry. He was an occultist, an astrologer and a black magician combined. A very close friend, an admirer of mine, said, "How I wish you would come and see this occultist." I said, "I do not care to see an occultist. If it is an occultist, I don't want to go." But my friend was adamant in his request, so I went to see the occultist at his hotel. When I went to his room, I just stood at the door while the occultist was sitting in a chair. What he saw in my eyes God knows. But he was so shocked that he sank onto the table and could not open his eyes for five minutes. He could not look at my eyes. He was crying and crying as if somebody had just saved his life. Then he rose and came to me with folded hands and said, "At this hour of my life, you have come. God gave me occult powers but I used them only on women and on wine. I used them so that people would appreciate and admire me and touch my feet. But I see in you a real flood of spiritual powers."

Then what did he do? He said to me, "I am not worthy of touching your feet, but I am touching your feet only to be pardoned, only to be blessed." He touched my feet and showed his devotion in many other ways.

When a spiritual Master stands before an occultist, the occultist, if he is a sincere man, will simply cry. He will weep because of the way he has misused his power. The spiritual life is flooded with purity and peace, and this peace and purity can easily swallow all the poisons of the occult world.

Question: Guru, you said that beings in the occult planes can use occult power in a way that could harm human beings. Are there actual beings that do this, or is it only the so-called black magicians? And how do they exert influence over people, especially spiritual aspirants?

Sri Chinmoy: No, black magicians are human beings who live among us on earth. The other beings are not human beings; they are beings in the vital plane. Sometimes they take the form of a tiny ant; sometimes they take a form as huge as an elephant. During our unconscious life they enter into us, and then they try to do negative things. Although people are practising the spiritual life, through jealousy or some other weakness, dark forces very often enter into them. Then these people fall spiritually and are often unable to regain their lost height until some future lifetime.

The Spirit World

Question: What are spirits or vital beings?

Sri Chinmoy: Some were once part of a human being, but some are only part of the universal existence. These entities do not want the soul's light. These beings get pleasure in creating mischief and destruction.

We cannot say that these forces are mental hallucinations. In the West we use the terms 'hallucination' and 'superstition.' We know that superstition and hallucination exist, but these beings also exist in the world of reality. I have seen them with my own eyes, as have other members of my own family, as well as our servants and neighbours. And I have dealt with them with my own light and spiritual power.

Question: Would these vital beings be frightened of your transcendental picture? And would it chase them off if they attacked us, let us say while we were walking down the street?

Sri Chinmoy: Believe me, if they see the transcendental picture and if the transcendental picture is operating at that time, they will be frightened. The trouble is that you will not think of the transcendental picture at that time. When you are attacked, you will be shocked, and the picture will not occur to you. But if the victim is receiving light from the transcendental picture, then they will be terribly frightened and are bound to leave. If the person receives, only then will the force go away. If my transcendental picture is there and somebody sees it who is not in any way my disciple, if he does not care for me, then it is just a picture. He will not receive light from it, and the forces will not be afraid.

If somebody has become a victim to these forces and you show him an ordinary picture, even if he has faith in that picture, it will not protect him. First of all, the person will not have enough faith in that particular picture if it is not my transcendental picture. Second, even if he does have faith in the picture, divinity will not come from there. The protective power of light works in a specific way. In this chair there is a soul, and in my body there is also a soul. But there is a great difference between the soul that I have in my body and the soul that the chair has. It is true that in a carrot there is God, and in a pencil there is God. But how much divinity is there in that carrot or in that pencil? If the victim looks at the transcendental picture and is able to receive from it, the vital being will have to leave. It will be terribly frightened of the light and power that will flow into the victim from the picture.

Forces attack, but protection is always there. The best thing to do is to think of protection first thing in the morning every day, when you pray and meditate.

Question: Is there any way for somebody – not somebody in the spiritual life but an ordinary person – to fight if a spirit attacks them? Is there anything that they could do? In the movies like Dracula and others they have the cross and all these religious things that will stop a ghost from hurting them.

Sri Chinmoy: It is good if one can show something like that. If a hostile spirit, an evil spirit, attacks, the most effective defence is always to use purity. These forces cannot tolerate purity.

If someone has been attacked and is helpless, occultists can do something to help them. I have also done this. First, they make a circle and then they enter into the soul of the person who is the victim. The soul can give the occultist a message; the soul has the omnipotent power to bring forward right in front of the occultist the actual image of that particular ghost or evil spirit. The soul, like an x-ray machine, will bring it forward and say, "Here is the one; this is the evil spirit that has attacked me." Then the occultist will immediately write down, or paint or somehow capture just the impression of the spirit on a piece of paper. He need not be an artist – far from it. Then he uses some occult formula and crosses the whole face with the help of the soul. When he does this, the spirit that was inside the victim leaves. The person may be unconscious; he may be vomiting or behaving strangely. Usually the victim of an evil spirit is terribly afraid of water, and also of his friends or relatives. Anything that he sees frightens him. But when the occultist uses his power, immediately the victim is released. In serious cases, when the victim does not get any help from a competent occultist, the doctors will give injections and do many things. The victim will remain in the hospital for three, four, five days before he dies, and most of the time he will be in a coma.

Question: Does this happen often?

Sri Chinmoy: I have known and seen about ten or eleven cases. Not that I have dealt with them, but I have seen the kinds of things that happen. Most of the time occultists deal with these things. In India there are some people who are not occultists at all, but they know something of the vital world and they deal with the evil forces in a very crude way. Their crude way is very bad. They start striking the victim violently. When I was six or seven years old, I had a neighbour who became a victim. A village exorcist came and began striking him mercilessly with a piece of wood. The man cried and screamed, but the exorcist said, "It is by striking him that I am actually exorcising the evil spirit." Now the exorcist was successful, as they often are, but that was a very crude way.

Question: Does this happen more in one part of the world than in another? There are more occultists in India than there are in America, so does this happen more there?

Sri Chinmoy: I have no idea. I have read a few books, and even in America it seems that this happens quite often.

Question: But they don't recognise it in America.

Sri Chinmoy: No, they don't recognise it in America. In America many people who have been attacked by a hostile force simply end up in a hospital because the cause of their malady is not understood. In Indian villages it is accepted as a daily occurrence. That is why between one and three o'clock in the afternoon children are forbidden to go out. If they have to go, they go in a group; they do not go out alone. Between one and three in the afternoon is the worst time.

Question: How does the spirit take possession of a person? How does the spirit gain access to the person's consciousness? Do they just go in?

Sri Chinmoy: They have the power in the vital world. They can easily do it while you are walking down the street or any time. And why just spirits? Human thought can also enter. If just now you have good thoughts, very powerful thoughts, with those powerful thoughts you can enter into someone else very powerfully. You are sending thought waves to someone, and he may see an actual being before him, as if in a dream. This being can take any form you will it to. From thought we can create form, for thought is very powerful. When the Yogis use their willpower or thought, immediately they give form to it. The story about stealing the eggplant* – do you think that it is just a cock-and-bull story, that it has no reality in it? That story is absolutely authentic. The woman who kept appearing all the time and the child and all that – these all came from thought waves, from the willpower of the Master. The Yogi used his willpower and immediately it took form.

---

* "Safe in the Master's Compassionate Concern," from *In Search of a Perfect Disciple*, a collection of short stories by Sri Chinmoy.

Question: I would like to know the difference between soul and spirit. I know that they are two entirely different things, but I cannot understand the difference.

Sri Chinmoy: A spirit, as the term is used in the West, is a vital entity, and it is usually not good. The soul, which embodies God, is deep inside us; it is part of the Self. Through the soul we enter into our all-pervading divinity. When we use the term 'soul,' it refers to a spark of the Self, the Omniscient and the Omnipotent.

A spirit, as we use the term here, refers to a vital entity which is unsatisfied or dissatisfied when the person dies, and which stays in the vital world for some time. There are many, many disturbing, obstructing, conflicting forces that take the form of spirits.

These spirits try to create disharmony, division and so forth. This is their function.

Spirits sometimes will also help someone gather information in the vital world about what is happening there or what is going to happen tomorrow or the day after. They have this capacity

The Spirit World

because the vital world is higher than the physical world. If you climb up a tree and look down from the top, you have a wider view and can see everything more clearly. From the vital world it is easier to observe the happenings of the physical world. But from the physical world it is very difficult to enter into the vital world. Occult practice or spiritism is involved here.

Very often spirits say to someone that they will bring their parents or their dearest ones to visit the bereaved person. I wish to say that people who listen to these spirits are committing a great blunder, because the spirits do not actually bring the soul of that particular person, their dearest and nearest. Rather, they bring dissatisfied, hungry entities from the vital world.

There are some spirits that take possession of the existence of the people who deal with them. The outer beings of these people allow the spirits to enter into them, with the result that they become possessed. Sometimes these people predict many things which may or may not happen. Unfortunately, however, this does not bring them into the spiritual life. After a few years the spirits say, "Now give me payment. I gave you name and fame. You did not know anything about the past or future. I showed you, so now you have to give me payment." What can he give? His name and fame cannot bring joy to the hungry spirits, so the spirits strangle him. Many, many black magicians and people who deal with spirits have been strangled or killed. I know because I have been near quite a few of these cases.

To come back to the term 'spirit,' in India we use the term with a capital S. and it means something different from what it means in the West. This Spirit is the masculine form of God which does not enter into the field of creation. It is the unmanifest Beyond, the Self. When we enter into the inner life and make spiritual progress, realising ourselves and liberating ourselves from fear, doubt and limitations, we gain a free access to the Spirit. There we achieve our own identity with the cosmic vision and reality. This conception of Spirit is not used in the West. In the West we use the term 'spirit' to refer to spiritism and to beings in the vital world.

Question: If a spirit comes to you, how can you tell if it is a good spirit or a bad one?

Sri Chinmoy: When good spirits come to you, you will always feel the fragrance of a flower. Even if there is no flower in the room, you will smell the fragrance of flowers or incense, and you will get joy. But when bad spirits come near you, you will always feel a kind of fear or anxiety or uneasy sensation in the room, and in your body. Just before they come you may have been very pure, but the bad spirits make your mind impure.

Question: Can a spirit help a person?

Sri Chinmoy: Yes. Parents may come during a dream and tell you to do something good, or they will tell you the future, or they may simply warn you that something is going to happen. My mother died over twenty years ago, and now she is in heaven. Hundreds of times she has come and helped me. Sometimes when I have misplaced something, and I am disturbed because I need that thing, my mother appears before me. Just as I see you in a physical form, I can see her, touch her. Then she tells me, "Look, it is there in that drawer." I say, "No, it cannot be there because I have not used that drawer. I never use it." But that is where I find it.

In India they say that if you put something down with your left hand, it will take hours of searching before you find it. Of course, there is another method. When I misplace something, if I concentrate I can find out immediately where it is.

Question: I read a booklet which says that every person has some guides connected to him and the person can pray to these guides. Is this true?

Sri Chinmoy: Yes, everyone has not only one, but two or three guides. In India we call them presiding deities. And also, our parents or relatives who are attached to us, after they have left the body, help and guide and pray for us. If they still have any feeling for us from that plane, they help. It is easier for them to pray for us than for us to pray for them, because they are on a higher level than we are.

Question: If we burn incense and candles, does this make it easier for us to invoke spirits?

Sri Chinmoy: When I used to have a pain in my feet, my sisters used to see a white figure massaging my feet. They did not see the actual face, but only a shadowy form. I could see the full face, however, and everything else. I told my sisters not to touch the spirit because it was extremely pure. I asked them to burn incense and candles and set out flowers. Whenever a spirit comes you have to do these things; otherwise it would be very difficult for the spirit to stay with you. Although you may be the purest man on earth, the spirits will find you always full of impurity. But if there is a flower, incense and a candle, then they will find it easier to remain.

Sri Ramakrishna, one of our great spiritual figures, after he had left the body, once went to the house of one of his devotees. The devotee wanted him to stay for a considerable time, but Sri Ramakrishna said, "Here, out of my infinite boundless love, I have come to you, but I see that you are so impure. You should keep incense burning in your room. When I come and stay in this place, it is like sleeping on a bed of thorns. How do you expect me to sleep on a bed of thorns?"

Question: Why do flowers and the burning of incense help to bring good spirits back?

Sri Chinmoy: It allows them to stay peacefully. It purifies the atmosphere. It is their food; it is a kind of fruit to them. You torture the spirits if your room is not clean when you invoke them, even though your body and your mind may be clean. You may be thinking of God and you feel you are pure, but if your room is not pure, it is torture for the spirits.

Question: Guru, how did the hostile forces originate?

Sri Chinmoy: They are all dissatisfied or unsatisfied beings. Some of them never took human birth; others were human beings once. And when they were human beings, they quarrelled and fought and murdered people and did all kinds of unspeakable things. They were not satisfied by any experience they had. Even by killing hundreds of people they could not have been satisfied. Satisfaction is not in their life.

Question: Will there ever be a time when there won't be any hostile forces anywhere?

Sri Chinmoy: There will be a time. It will take millions of years, but certainly God will not remain imperfect forever. He cannot. He must perfect them someday.

Question: When you fight, Guru, do you have an army?

Sri Chinmoy: Yes, many armies.

Question: Is it your inner beings, or is it other beings also?

Sri Chinmoy: My inner beings fight with me and for me.

Question: Is the weapon concentration?

Sri Chinmoy: It is not concentration. Spiritual Masters keep some solid power, which they can use if they want. It is not the power of concentration. It is like the strength you have in your arms. You do not use it at every moment. Similarly, inside me I have solid strength; it is there already. When the time comes, I just use it. It is like having thousands of dollars in the bank; it is up to you to use it. You can use one cent or the whole thousand dollars. But why should you use one thousand dollars or even one cent if there is no need? If there is need, a divine need, in most cases the decision to use this power comes from the Supreme.

Question: Guru, do you ever call on the disciples to fight these battles?

Sri Chinmoy: Still I don't have that kind of disciple. You will be like that one day. Then I will use you gladly, very gladly. When I was somebody's disciple, I used to participate in hundreds and hundreds of these battles. Then what? The following morning I received no recognition. Only once, when I did something most extraordinary, when my own Guru did not dare to do that kind of thing, on the following day the Guru told the person what I had done. But usually he would not give me credit on the physical plane.

Question: Guru, when you talk about fighting a hostile force, is it a question of bringing down something and injecting it? Or is it actually a kind of struggle that you are engaged in? When you fight a hostile force, how does that differ from just meditating and bringing down light and peace?

Sri Chinmoy: In meditation we invoke peace and very devotedly try to receive what descends. But when we meet a hostile force, it is like a battlefield. There we must blindly kill. There we do not think of father, mother, brother. There we have to act absolutely like a mad elephant. No, 'mad elephant' is not the correct word. When spiritual people fight the hostile forces, it is like hundreds of lions fighting. There it is not like bringing anything down. It is real fighting.

Question: What is it like when you fight in the inner world?

Sri Chinmoy: How can I tell you? In the vital world there are many, many destructive forces. Now most of you have not even seen a ghost. God does not want to show you a ghost. But these forces in the vital worlds are infinitely more powerful and more frightening than a ghost. They are extremely ugly and filthy and, at the same time, unthinkably strong. When you see them you do not even want to fight. You feel that it is better to surrender immediately. It is not that they are so beautiful and luminous that you want to die at their feet. No! As soon as you see them you think it is impossible to defeat them, so you say the best thing is to surrender and just peacefully die.

Question: Have you ever been possessed by a spirit?

Sri Chinmoy: Spirits come and try to possess spiritual Masters, but they cannot possess us. We do not allow them to. It is God's Will that we fight them.

Once when I was twenty-one years old, six spirits came and attacked me. I was in my bed and I started to fight with them. By God's Grace those spirits had to leave, but they returned later. It was around three a.m., and there was such a commotion that all the members of the house – there were eleven or twelve of them – came down. Only my brother, who was there in my room in a bed right next to mine, could see that I was fighting with something and talking in another language. He did not know the meaning of what I was saying, but he wrote what he heard when I was arguing and fighting with them. Afterwards he asked me the meaning of it, but I had forgotten everything. Later I concentrated and meditated and told him the meaning of these foreign words.

These spirits were evil spirits. Very often evil spirits try to take away our spiritual power in our unguarded moments. It is not only spiritual power that they take; if you have honesty, simplicity or, especially, purity, they try to take it away. Purity they take first, because they know that if purity is gone from somebody, then that person cannot progress any further. If one wants to have something lasting in one's spiritual life, then one must have purity first.

Question: Guru, do things happen in the West such as evil spirits entering people and then everybody thinks it is some medical defect? For instance, could some psychiatric cases really be cases of evil forces that have entered?

Sri Chinmoy: Yes. In the West, there are many like this whom I have seen under psychiatric treatment. One of my first disciples had actually been attacked by an evil force, but her mother thought that it was a mental breakdown and put her in a hospital in the Bronx for a year or two. She became practically insane there. One day another disciple told me about her and I felt very sorry. I was in Manhattan at the time and I went to see her. She had been there for some time, suffering and not making any progress, and was in very bad condition. They thought that she had lost her sanity and needed psychiatric treatment, but I saw clearly that she had been attacked by an undivine force. She didn't know me well at that time; she had only heard about me casually. But I did help her and a few days later she was released. Twice after that we held meditations and I gave talks at her house. One time when I was about to start my meditation there, her cat came and fell at my feet, and told me inwardly that it wanted to have a human incarnation. Everybody was so surprised because all of a sudden the cat came and fell flat at my feet and looked at me so fixedly.

Question: If you hadn't helped her, would the forces have stayed for the rest of her life or would they have just left after a while?

Sri Chinmoy: I have no idea what would have happened in her case. Perhaps it would have lasted for quite a few years, and then if the forces saw that she was getting weaker and weaker, they would have left. They would leave, not out of mercy, but because they had destroyed the person. Then they would go to somebody else. And it is not that as soon as they leave the person becomes all right. No! If they have severely damaged or permanently ruined a person, then they can go to some other person and try to create problems for him. If the spirit has not totally destroyed the victim, then there is a possibility that he can be cured. But after total destruction, at that time it is a hopeless case.

Question: What happens to that soul in its next incarnation? Is it ruined?

Sri Chinmoy: The soul is not ruined. But the poor soul does not get enough opportunity in this incarnation to make progress, to manifest its divinity.

Question: How can you tell the difference between someone who wants power because he is possessed by one of these beings and someone who wants power because it is his nature, because he is not spiritually developed?

Sri Chinmoy: If one has the ability, the easiest thing is to concentrate on the soul. Then one can see whether the person has become a victim of these wrong forces or if his own vital being is craving for power. Let us consider a child. We should feel purity in a child's face; by nature a child should be sweet and loveable. But instead of that, if we see a child is always breaking things, fighting and full of aggression, we will know that this child has been possessed by something. In some cases, the child is born possessed in this way and when he grows up his very nature is to fight and seek to conquer. He always wants others to be behind him or at his feet. With a child, one can easily tell in this way. And if one can concentrate on someone's soul, one will immediately know if that person has been possessed by another being or not.

Question: Is there a way to combat these beings?

Sri Chinmoy: Yes, by bringing in peace. Peace is the best antidote. When peace enters into these beings, they die immediately. It is like poison to them, for this restless world is terribly afraid of peace. If we can throw peace into the persons who have become victims of these aggressive life-forces, then peace immediately swallows their aggression. Parents can easily solve the problem by concentrating on the hearts of their young children and bringing peace into them. There is no other solution; only peace will solve the problem.

Question: Why is it necessary for a soul that has left the body many years ago to ask for a material thing, in this case a skull (referring to a story about a ghost shaking the bed of someone who had taken an old skull from a cemetery)?

Sri Chinmoy: Ordinary souls have a malicious attitude of revenge. If they cannot take revenge on someone while they are on earth, they want to take it from the other world. They are not satisfied, and it is immaterial to them whether they act on a friend or on an enemy. They take revenge because they feel that they are gaining something. They get pleasure in this and are merciless. I know many cases similar to this story you told. These souls ask just for minor things – for a dollar, for example – and if they don't get it, what do they do? They enter into your subtle nerves and upset your whole system. I know of a young boy whose friend died. This boy owed the friend the equivalent of a dime in Indian currency. For seven nights his friend came back saying, "Give me my money." The boy said, "I am ready to give it back to you, but how will you take it?" The friend said, "No, give me, give me my money." At the end of the week the boy's health was shattered and he was bedridden for two months.

If you have a servant – a maid, for example – and the maid dies, if she wants to take revenge, she can remain in the vital world for a few months or a few years. From there her spirit may create many problems. But then, everything is limited; she cannot go on torturing you forever.

You have no idea how one particular woman suffered when her first husband committed suicide. Two or three hours after the wedding took place, he got the brilliant idea to kill himself. How she suffered from it for five, six, seven years – perhaps even more. Every day she was attacked, threatened, frightened, tortured in so many ways. I was in India at that time and I did not know her, but a friend of mine asked me to help her. I used my power, and after so many years of torturing her, the spirit finally left her alone.

We think that as soon as the soul leaves the body it becomes generous, pure, forgiving; but this is not so. If it were that way, we would always welcome death. We would say to death, "The moment you accept me I will be free from all bondage." But it is not like that. The standard that we achieve in this life is a stepping stone. In our next incarnation we have to start with our present achievement. If we have cultivated forgiveness, love and sacrifice in this incarnation, then on the strength of our forgiveness, love and sacrifice we will go a step ahead in our next incarnation.

People who try to take revenge on their friends or acquaintances after their soul has left the body are really making great blunders. They are hampering their future incarnation, because they are not leaving the vital world. They are staying in the vital world and entering into the gross physical world to threaten, to frighten or to give some news. If they tried instead to enter into the mental world or the plane of intuition or the higher mind or overmind or the soul's region, then they would make real progress, but they do not.

When that man whom you referred to in your question took home the skull, he put himself in contact with the vital forces. And he was inviting trouble by doing that. When I was nine or ten, I went to a place where I saw a skull. I saw a few words in Sanskrit written on the skull. Later, while I was going back home, I saw inwardly that in those very few words a long letter was written, and in this letter the deceased person was telling how his wife and children had been cruel and unjust to him. If I had brought the skull home, I would have had the same fate as the man you referred to in your question. Even though I was not involved with the deceased person, just because I showed interest in that particular skull I would have been bothered by him.

Question: But what happens to these souls? They are not free but are still somehow bound to their former lives.

Sri Chinmoy: If a spiritual figure wants to show compassion, then he liberates them, he frees them from the vital plane. He tells them that they are causing misery not only for their relatives and friends but also for themselves. He tells them that they have no future and no light ahead if they continue like this. But unless a Master helps, these souls often remain in this deplorable condition for many, many years.

Question: How do they ever get out of it?

Sri Chinmoy: They get out when they finally realise that there are also higher worlds, which they can have. In the vital world, also, one must aspire to go beyond, to go higher. If there is no aspiration, then one has to stay. Even in this world, if one has no aspiration one will make absolutely no progress during his life. He will come and remain as a most ordinary human being, perhaps for many lifetimes. There are many human beings who act like animals. Why is that? Because they do not even have the aspiration to go beyond their animal consciousness.

Question: What are ghosts? Are they the vital beings of dead people?

Sri Chinmoy: Most of them are dissatisfied vital beings. Satisfied ones do not do these things. That is why in India, people observe quite a few rites when someone dies. For one month, they actually feed the deceased. If somebody dies, they keep all kinds of food in front of their house for one month after, thinking that the man who has died is still hungry. We used to keep food for our father and mother. Very often a dog would come and eat the food, and sometimes we became annoyed. But the village brahmin gave us sound advice. He said, "Your father has taken the form of a dog and the dog is eating the food." I observed it at least six or seven times with tears in my eyes thinking, "Oh, my father is eating." The dog was eating the food and I used to look at the dog with such affection, because the brahmin had told us that the dog was eating on behalf of my father. Such village beliefs! I have seen it with my own eyes. When my father died and when my mother died, we observed this ritual for one month and then, after a month, we believed they were not hungry any more.

Question: Is there any truth to stories about haunted houses?

Sri Chinmoy: Absolutely! Let me tell you about an experience of mine not long ago in Connecticut. We spent a few nights at a particular lady's house. When she told me her house was haunted, I did not pay much attention to it. But at night the spirits came. I think there were three spirits involved: a father and two sons. It was a very long story. They screamed and screamed, trying to frighten me. The first night I didn't take it seriously, but the second night it was really terrible, and I had to take it seriously. They bent a branch of a tree so it came right into my window, breaking the window. The branch came and practically pushed me out of bed. Then I said, "All right! Your time has come," and I threw them out.

Question: Could the lady hear them too, Guru, or just you?

Sri Chinmoy: Anybody could hear them. She heard them many times. Her daughter used to get frightened, and sometimes she even fainted.

Question: Did they know who you were? Were they doing that on purpose?

Sri Chinmoy: No. They didn't know that I was a spiritual man or anything. They just thought that somebody was staying there, so they did it.

Question: If you hadn't thrown these spirits out, would they have left on their own?

Sri Chinmoy: Of their own accord, spirits do not decide to go. Once they have occupied a place, it is like a hostile force; they occupy a territory and one has to work very hard to get them out. I have done it in a few places. Some people pray to God and then God helps them.

Question: Can everyone see ghosts, or just some people?

Sri Chinmoy: If they take a form, the spirits can be seen by everyone. They can take a beautiful or an ugly form. When I was only twelve years old, one of our servants was attacked by a ghost. He was about twenty-three years old. Around noon or one o'clock, he was walking along the street when suddenly, from a tree, the stupid fellow saw a beautiful woman calling for help. When he went to help her, she started kicking him with her knees. The boy fell down and fainted. Afterwards he was taken to a hospital and they tried all kinds of medicine on him. How he suffered! It was not a mental hallucination or anything.

Usually the female spirits are more mischievous than the masculine ones. Female ones come with a very beautiful form and call someone, and when the person goes, they kick him like anything. One evening my elder brother and his friend were walking together near a bamboo tree. Bamboo trees are very tall, and they saw that this tree was bending very low. My brother actually saw a woman in the tree, but his friend did not. It was not his third eye or anything that let him see the woman while his friend did not; it was just that his friend was not paying attention. His friend was so delighted to see a bamboo tree bent to such an extent that he just grabbed hold of it. The tree snapped back up, and my brother's friend was thrown to the top of the tree. When he fell back down he broke his elbow and his shoulder. Nothing happened to my brother.

Question: Do these spirits have personal grudges against the people?

Sri Chinmoy: Not actually against any individual, but they are mischievous beings that get pleasure from doing such things.

Question: What about graveyards? Are there ghosts there?

Sri Chinmoy: In graveyards and in cremation grounds too, you can see how ghosts and evil forces fight and scream at night. People who live nearby can hear them. The place where we went the other day for a picnic, I saw many evil forces. Many people have committed suicide on that estate. Usually there are ghosts and evil forces moving around in an area where people have committed suicide.

Mediums and the Unseen World

Question: What is it that the spiritual mediums contact when they give messages? Whom or what are they speaking to?

Sri Chinmoy: They try to speak to the soul itself. If I want to see somebody's brother or father or mother who has died, I can see, I can speak to the soul. When you become Self-realised, you also can speak to your parents in that way if they are not on earth. If they are still in Heaven or in some other higher world, it is very easy to speak to the soul. If they have taken a new human incarnation, it becomes a little difficult, but we can still do it.

The soul has its own language. Just as we speak directly to a human being, we can speak directly to the soul. An ordinary man who is not realised also can speak to a soul if he has some connection with or control of a spirit in the vital plane. Information received through spirits, however, is often incorrect or imperfect. If somebody's father or mother has died and wants to take the trouble to help a son or daughter on earth, the spirit of the deceased, no matter where it is, can come and give messages. At any time, these spirits can concentrate on them, think of them and give the message. Even now there are most ordinary people who do not pray even for a second, but who nonetheless get messages from relatives in the soul's world. This process is in no way sure or certain, however. People who receive messages in this way are always at the mercy of the whims of their departed dear ones.

Question: How can one contact one's dear ones in the other world?

Sri Chinmoy: There are a few ways to contact dear ones who are not in this world. The easiest way, the way that you hear about all the time, is to go to a medium. The medium will tell you many stories about your relatives who are in Heaven.

Unfortunately, very often these stories have nothing to do with reality. Only rarely do mediums bring real inner messages from the soul. You have to know that when a person has left the body only a few days or a few months ago, or a year or two ago, then there is a possibility that the soul is still in the vital world. At that time, it is easier for the medium to bring down true messages. But when the soul enters into the mental world, intuitive world, psychic world and the soul's own proper world, which is infinitely higher than the vital world, at that time the messages that you get from the medium are all untrue.

Another way is to go to a real spiritual Master. If I go to the owner of a shop, a big shop, and ask him to do something, if he is pleased with me he will immediately do me the favour. But if I go to just a messenger boy or an ordinary clerk, I will see that his capacity is very, very limited. In the spiritual world, when one goes to a real Master, one finds that his capacity is unlimited. He is like the owner of the shop. He knows what he has, he knows where it is, and he can give anything he wants to anybody. But a medium is just like a clerk or messenger boy. He has very little power to give you what you want.

When a spiritual Master takes or brings the message, he enters into the soul of the person who is asking him for this favour, because this person's soul will know where the soul of his relative is right now. His mind does not know, his heart does not know, his vital does not know, his body does not know where the soul of the dear one has gone. But the soul knows. However, spiritual Masters usually do not like to carry this kind of message, because they feel it is all curiosity.

If a person has a sincere cry rather than just curiosity, he does not have to go to anybody if he wants to send a message to a departed friend or relative. His sincere prayer is infinitely more safe and sure than accepting someone else as his messenger. If he offers his message to God with his heart of prayer and his heart of meditation, God can easily carry his message to the person it is meant for. The heart that wants to pray immediately becomes one with God's Compassion. The heart that wants to meditate immediately becomes one with God's Light. If we contact God's Light and God's Compassion, then without fail our prayer, our meditation will reach the right person.

Now how do we know whether the person has received our message or not? We have to have faith. We go to a medium because we have faith in the medium. We go to a spiritual Master because we have faith in him. Why should we not also have faith in our own prayer? If we have no faith in the medium, even if the message is correct, we will not believe it. If we have no faith in the Master, even if he does everything right in front of us, we will say that it is all hallucination. If we have faith in our own prayer, our prayer has the capacity to become a pure child who will run lovingly toward his Father to get something. The moment the Father sees that His child has come running to Him with such love and faith, the Father will immediately give him everything.

If we cannot pray or meditate, if we do not care for a spiritual Master and have very little or no faith in a medium, then there is a practical way to send messages to our departed ones. We should note down about seven incidents in our life that have to do with that person. The incidents should be most soulful and intimate, anything that is still living in our heart. When we have seven incidents which are most intimate, most soulful, we must place them before ourselves one by one. Then we must take each incident and enter into it with our present life and present concern. Each incident is like a tiny dot.

When we enter into it with our present life-breath, we see that from a dot it becomes a big round circle. The intensity, the capacity of our life-breath immediately makes it bigger. Then the life-breath of that reality will enter into the universal reality and become one with the universal reality. When we clearly see that this is the universal reality, the face of the person in subtle physical form is bound to appear. If we are ordinary men, we will not be able to touch this subtle physical; if we are spiritual people, the subtle physical will be palpable, solid.

Here we have to be very practical. We have to have confidence in the world which is right in front of us. When we look into the universal reality and see the person's face, we will be able to offer our message. But we have to feel that those intimate moments are the only moments that existed between ourselves and our loved one. If any disturbance or any action which displeased us enters into our feeling for this person, then immediately we are ruined. We have to have the feeling that we would be willing to give our life for that person, and that he would also be willing to give his life for us. When we can feel that we each are ready to give our life for the other, at that time we can become consciously one with that person's life, and we can easily give or receive a message.

Question: If one tries to contact somebody who has departed from the world, then how can one be sure one has contacted that particular soul and not an evil spirit?

Sri Chinmoy: We have to know what kind of souls we are dealing with. If the person who has left the body is not a very evolved soul, there can very often be difficulties when we try to contact him. Very often destructive beings take beautiful, luminous forms from the vital world and come to us as our relatives.

If you want to know whether it is actually your relative or some other being, what should you do? You should pray to God with all your heart and soul to bring forward all of your purity. Then, when you feel that you have brought all your purity to the fore, you should look at the feet – not the face – of that being. If you are surcharged with purity, then immediately any evil being will disappear. Sometimes they literally burst and make a terrible noise.

If a spiritual Master is not of a very high order, sometimes the hostile forces will take his form. They stand in front of the disciple and say, "Do this! Don't do this!" The disciple listens and then everything goes wrong. In such cases, when the Master is still on earth, there should always be some means of identification for the disciple.

I know of a case in India where the hostile forces used to take the form of a particular spiritual Master and ask the disciples to commit suicide. "If you commit suicide, I will be able to give you liberation sooner," it would say. They tried to commit suicide even though the Master told them outwardly that he had never said that. These hostile forces are very clever. They play all kinds of tricks and make all kinds of mischief and destruction, but they have to surrender eventually to the Supreme's Power.

It is not possible for an ordinary human being to know whether he has contacted the real person or the wrong forces except by his conscience. Conscience comes to the fore and makes him feel immediately that this being is not the correct one. A child does not examine anyone mentally; he does not have the capacity. When two persons stand in front of him, he cannot distinguish which is real and which is not. But his heart or conscience makes him feel that one person is real and the other is unreal.

For an ordinary person, conscience will make him feel whether he has contacted the right person or not. For a spiritual person it will be easier. And for a Master, it takes not a second to tell whether the right being or an undivine being has come.

Question: Can a person lend his body so that a spirit can enter and talk through him?

Sri Chinmoy: It is possible. This is what mediums often try to do. It often happens spontaneously, especially in children. They speak to their parents and the parents observe that the children have a peculiar expression on their face, a different personality with a different way of expression. At that time the child is possessed by some other spirit.

Question: I had an experience in my childhood. In my home everybody played the piano, and as far back as I can remember, everybody has played the piano. One day when I was three years old I asked the maid to take me to the piano, and I started playing with both hands a tune that my mother had been playing the night before. What is the explanation of this?

Sri Chinmoy: It may have been a spirit playing through you and it may have been something else. Most probably, in your last life you acquired mastery in playing the piano and all of a sudden your intuition brought forward that experience, that mastery. Very often a child's intuition is at the fore. A child seldom does anything consciously. He does everything intuitively. A child speaks to God all the time even though he does not open his mouth. A constant communion is going on between the child and God.

Question: I didn't only play once; I played many times like this. What does this mean?

Sri Chinmoy: In that case it was the play of intuition, not a spirit. A spirit will not come too often to a child, because the gods that are guiding him will not allow it. If a spirit enters, very often it will try to damage something.

Question: What do you think of healing in relation to spirituality?

Sri Chinmoy: I wish to say a few words from the spiritual point of view about what I think of healing. Healing deserves special attention and, at the same time, special appreciation from spirituality. An ordinary healer heals a person in order to get name or fame or just because he has an inner urge to help humanity. But a spiritual person heals a particular person only when God asks him to or when he gets personal permission from God to do so.

When an ordinary healer heals a person, he is often affected by the disease or the ailment of the patient. Very often I come across people who have healed and then themselves become victims of those ailments that they have cured in some other people. Some actually die of the disease they have cured in others. But when a spiritual person cures someone, he cures with his soul's light. He enters into the sufferer with his soul's light, and he cures the person without becoming attached. There is a continuous cosmic flow in and through his life, and that continuous flow of cosmic energy enters into the patient from him. Then it is just as though light were permeating the entire body of the person who is suffering. So a spiritual person heals only when he is commanded by the Divine or when he gets special permission from the Divine. Then he becomes totally one with the sufferer on the strength of his soul's oneness, and cures with his soul's light.

Question: What is the relationship between automatic writing and mediums?

Sri Chinmoy: Real spirituality does not indulge in automatic writing and things like that. To go to a medium to find out what is happening in Heaven, on earth or in the vital world is not at all spiritual. Spirituality means constant aspiration to be totally unified with God. Spirituality means one's natural oneness with God. Real spirituality is absolutely normal and natural.

If somebody is interested in automatic writing and such things, you have to try to kindle the flame of aspiration in him. If he is very near and dear to you, he may listen to you. Try to make him see that it is he who has discovered the truth and not you who are unfolding the truth to him or injecting the truth into him. When one feels that one has discovered the truth oneself from within, it becomes normal and natural. This evening during your meditation, kindly try to enter into him and make him feel that it is he who has all of a sudden realised the truth that automatic writing is not really good, but that concentration, meditation and contemplation – which come from aspiration – are truly good. In that way you will be able to bring him to the right path. Please try inwardly and not outwardly.

Question: From your viewpoint is hypnosis acceptable or not, and why?

Sri Chinmoy: If one wants to realise the Truth, which is God, there is no necessity for hypnosis or self-hypnosis. What is necessary is peace, bliss and power. These things we can get through aspiration. By taking someone into the world of inconscience or to the subconscious plane through hypnosis, by making him aware of his past defects, imperfections and impurities, we are not able to help the person reach his ultimate goal. But by bringing down from above the things that can change and mould his life and make him a better person, we can be of much help to a person.

I have disciples in New York who indulge in hypnosis. But I say to them, "What do you want from yourselves? What do you expect from the other person? If you want the other person to be freed from misery, frustration and worry, then show him the light and do not ponder over his past failings or the defects that are preventing him from expanding his free consciousness."

If one wants peace, if one wants fulfilment, if one wants joy out of life, then spirituality is the immediate answer. Spirituality seems a very vague word. People call something spiritual when it is something which they cannot comprehend with their physical minds. Anything a little abstruse they think is spiritual. But spirituality is not something foreign; it is not something theoretical and unreal. It is something natural and practical, a practical achievement and realisation. Spirituality is something spontaneous, something that unites the inner life with the outer life. Spirituality can solve all human problems, inner and outer, as well as problems that are not yet even born in our life. Spirituality can solve these problems before they manifest themselves; it can enter into them and destroy them.

I feel that hypnosis is of no value. What is of value is aspiration – bringing down into the physical consciousness infinite peace, bliss and power through constant aspiration.

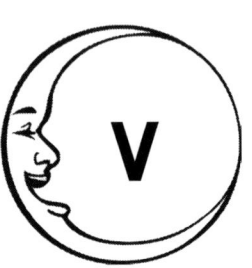

Man and the Universe

Question: Do you believe that there are people just like us here on most of the other planets?

Sri Chinmoy: The beings on other planets are all subtle. Although these beings can take any form, their subtle form will look like a human being, especially when they appear before us on earth. We feel that the subtle bodies that come before us are real, that they have flesh and bones and all, but actually they do not. Our human flesh is composed of five elements which these beings do not have. We can touch them and we will feel that they are solid. This is not a hallucination, but an absolute reality. But the sensation you have when you touch my flesh would be different from the sensation you would get if you touched the body of these beings. The difference is in perception.

Question: Do you believe there are beings from other planets who come to earth in flying saucers?

Sri Chinmoy: Yes, I do believe that there are other beings who come in flying saucers. There is much truth in what is said about them, but not the complete truth. It is wrong to say that they are superior to us. They are altogether different beings, not like human beings at all. They act from a different plane and do not have an ordinary mind like human beings have, but that does not mean that they are fools.

These beings are luminous and very beautiful. They can reveal any form they like to the human mind. But while on earth they take human form just to show that it is possible. But if we could go to their own world, we would see that very often they take the form of a flower, a bird or an angel.

There are human beings who can consciously go to another world during their sleep, even though they may not be spiritually aspiring. These people, however, are not totally human. They come from other worlds but take a human incarnation in order to see our world. One of my disciples in New York is one of these people. When I bless her and look at her face during meditation, I immediately see that she comes from a spirit world, a world of angels. Her soul is very much in tune with that world and she very often goes there. These souls from other worlds, who have taken human form, are often found in Vermont, in Canada and in Southern India.

The language of these beings when they are not in human form is altogether different from ours. We cannot speak to them in their own tongue, but we can speak to them if we know the language of the soul, because these beings also have a soul. They come here out of curiosity to see what earth looks like and what is actually happening here. They come from another planet just to investigate, not to seek help from us or to get any benefit here. In our case we want to evolve and we want to go to God, so we seek illumination. They cannot help us and we cannot help them. We have this material world; it is self-sufficient. Their worlds are also self-sufficient. But at the same time, they are like beggars because in their worlds they do not have God-realisation.

If a being from that world wants God-realisation, Self-discovery, it has to take a human body, whereas we do not need any other form to realise God. This is the advantage that we have. Although we are full of suffering, limitation and ignorance here, this physical world offers the only possibility to realise the Supreme. Beings from every other place must come down into this world if they want to realise God. God is available only here. With God-realisation, you can go to any place; in every place there is God. But full realisation you must attain here on this planet earth, and nowhere else.

Question: Is man unique in the whole universe?

Sri Chinmoy: In the whole universe, in all of God's creation, man is unique because next to man is total perfection, complete unveiling consciousness. Man is unique because he has the absolute potentiality to realise God, and when we realise God, who can be superior?

There are thousands of cosmic gods. If I get a headache, and if I pray to a certain cosmic god, that god will take away my headache. If I get a stomach ache, I have to pray to a different god. But these gods are not superior to me. They are all supernatural entities in the vital world with capacities higher than those of ordinary men. These beings are usually good, but they are all finished products. They do not make any progress because they do not care to enter into the world for the transformation of their nature.

Question: So they cannot become God, they cannot reach God?

Sri Chinmoy: No, they cannot. In that world they are stuck at one point. They have to come into a human body and accept human life like us with its bondage, suffering, suppression and humiliation if they wish to evolve.

Question: So we are more evolved than they?

Sri Chinmoy: Yes, in the sense of our aspiration toward God-realisation we are more evolved. But at the same time, they are in a world of joy and exquisite delight, which we do not have. Our joy is very limited. Often what we call joy here is really only pleasure. The fact is that they are happier; but happiness is not God-realisation.

There are some cosmic gods who try, out of jealousy, to prevent human beings from going beyond their [the gods'] own achievements and attaining Self-realisation, for human beings can have full realisation, while the cosmic gods have only a limited consciousness. Most of the spiritual figures who have attained Self-realisation say that in the beginning the cosmic gods helped them in their spiritual progress. But when they tried to go beyond the limited domain of the cosmic deities, they met with vehement resistance from those very gods. But if the aspirant is very, very powerful, and if he is very, very intense, the Grace of the Supreme descends, and the aspirant is able to go beyond the minor gods. We must not give much importance to the cosmic gods, or angels, as we call them in the West. No, we have to go beyond them, beyond them. They are not human beings; their life-process is different from ours.

These gods are sometimes cursed by the aspirants and, if they are cursed, they have to take a human incarnation. There is always anger, in man as well as in the gods. When the gods get angry with an aspirant, they will curse his family. At that time, if the aspirant is really strong, he will literally refuse the curse. Then the god will have to come to the human world and will have to undergo suffering. These things really happen, even in the high worlds of the cosmic gods.

Question: Will science ever discover the soul?

Sri Chinmoy: Science will never, never discover the soul. It is not possible, because the soul comes from a region far beyond the domain of science. The soul can only be realised on the strength of one's identification or oneness with the Absolute. This oneness refers to a plane of consciousness. But science does not deal with planes of consciousness; it deals only with the facts that it gets from the physical world. Consciousness is something which science is not approaching and cannot approach.

Science can investigate certain spiritual phenomena. Some Yogis can stop their breathing and stay buried underground for hours and days without their heart functioning. One can consciously stop one's breathing and the functioning of the heart, but science cannot believe this. Science says, "Without the heartbeat, how can one live?"

There are many things science can discover, many marvels, but science cannot go beyond the range of the senses. Beyond the range of the senses there are planes of consciousness where one can see the soul playing, moving, dancing and doing many other things. If a spiritual man wants to, he can easily see the soul of any person. There are many things that are not visible in the outer plane and yet are absolutely real. If you have seen your soul or your psychic being, how can science deny it? We adore science because science has discovered many, many things. But we cannot deny the things that spiritual persons have discovered and have made others see.

Question: Do you think God will help the hand of those doctors who are transplanting hearts from dead people into sick people? Do you think that this will be a practice in the future?

Sri Chinmoy: I wish to say that God is helping everyone on earth. Why only through transplantation? When we are in ignorance, God is helping us; when we are in wisdom, God is helping us. When we do something wrong or we see others do wrong, you may say that God does not help at that time. But even then sometimes there is protection. We are not punished all at once.

The world is constantly evolving. The doctor is now trying to conquer death. The scientist is trying to conquer death. The spiritual aspirant is trying to conquer death. We are attacking death from every angle. When we have conquered death, we will become immortal. But from the strict spiritual point of view, I wish to say that immortality will come through aspiration and not through transplantation. When a soul takes a human body, it brings its own particular heart, its own particular mind, its own particular vital, its own particular physical. Now when you replace something, you introduce a foreign element. Anything that comes from elsewhere cannot be mine; it cannot be my own possession. But by using foreign things, scientists have discovered that they can prolong the life process for five, ten or even twenty years.

What we are doing with heart transplants is, to some extent, unnatural. It lets us delay death, prolong life, but it will not allow us to immortalise our physical existence. For immortality we have to have

a different body, a different consciousness,
a different illumination.

Medical science is trying to conquer death, but actual physical immortality will come into existence only through aspiration and God's conscious Will. If you feel that medical science will eventually conquer death then I must say that you are mistaken. Death will be conquered when each individual someday possesses a different consciousness, and that consciousness will come only after liberation and Self-realisation. We will have at that time a different body, a divinised body, a transformed body.

A day will come when a different order of beings will inhabit the earth. They will not have the same organs that we now have, and they will not have so many organs. They will be a completely different race. They will not be limited by the body-consciousness at all. The body will be a more subtle body, which will have no need of all the internal functions and organs that we have now. It will be a divine body – very luminous, very beautiful, very strong and powerful. The body will also be adaptable. If something is thrown at it, like an arrow, the body would have the power to repel the object without letting it come near. And if the object did come near, it would go right through the body without causing any harm. The body will have many capabilities that it does not have now.

And there will be no differentiation of the sexes, and no need for reproduction and the mating of male and female. All souls will incarnate through occult means. The actual union will take place in the psychic world, and from this psychic world the souls will take a body. These souls will not come to life through the mother's body. And souls will be able to call other souls to incarnate when they want them. However, the hour for all this has not yet struck and it will take a long time to come.

Question: What happens when a woman's heart is transplanted into a man's body?

Sri Chinmoy: At birth we inherit the constitutional make-up of both our parents. For example, we may have a physical body which is phlegmatic or perhaps highly nervous. The body has its own rhythm, and the heart is part of this rhythm. If the heart of a young girl who is very light and dynamic were transplanted into a man who is very heavy and lethargic, for example, his body would have a tendency to reject it. Doctors know that the physical cells of one's body will not tolerate any substance that is foreign and will automatically reject any foreign organ. They tell us that only the physical organ of a very close relative who has the same genes, the same cell make-up, will be tolerated. So, in the case of the heart transplant I was speaking of, the man's body would not find it compatible; it would see it as a foreign element and throw it off. Since the heart is the physical organ of life, it is very important that it should be of the same physical make-up as the rest of the body.

This brings up another point. The heart is the seat of the emotions and we always identify our deeper feelings with the heart. We say, "I love you with all my heart." And although the physical heart is just an organ, the emotions – what we call the vital or emotional nature of man – are invisibly housed in this heart area. This vital nature is actually housed in the middle of the chest, but not in the physical heart itself. Even so, whenever one person's heart is transplanted into another person's body, a certain emotional confusion and disorientation are bound to take place.

I am not actually in favour of heart transplantation, for it impedes the spontaneous flow of life-energy. Also, the physical sheath, which is composed of five elements, finds the transplantation a tangible intrusion of a foreign element in subtle ways that medical science will not understand. Medical science can prolong a person's life by transplanting a heart, but mere prolongation of life is of no avail when one's inner aspiration for the perfection of one's own body is lacking. A real aspirant will not be able to aspire for a higher purpose with the potentialities and capacities of a different heart.

Question: I was wondering how the souls of identical twins are related, or if they are not at all?

Sri Chinmoy: Very interesting question! There is no hard and fast rule. Generally, they were not close to each other in the soul's world. Sometimes their souls are related, but not because of some intimate connection in past incarnations. Sometimes the souls come to punish each other. In the field of manifestation, the twins have no idea that this is true; they may, in fact, become friends. But in the soul's region, the twin souls are not at all complementary to each other. They say, "If you enter into this family, then I am also entering – and not at a different time, but at the same time. Then I will see what you can do." I have seen this as the inner reason many times, I must say. But when the parents show infinite love and affection to the twins, and when they try to show the same amount of love to both, the souls of the twins get a kind of spontaneous wish to be loveable or to have a common cause, a common destination. But these things – the common goal, common realisation, common fulfilment – never occurred to them while they were in the soul's region. Here I must give credit to the parents, for the parents have considerably changed their children's natures. And the children eventually get a better life, a better understanding and a better achievement and fulfilment.

Question: Is it possible to meet your twin soul later on in life? Do certain people have soul mates?

Sri Chinmoy: Soul mates and twin souls are not one. A soul mate is one with whom you have a very close soul's affinity. You now live in Hartford, but in New York there may be someone who is your soul's closest friend. When I concentrate on you people,

I see there are quite a few who have a soul's affinity with one another.

I see also in Puerto Rico that there are some who have this soul's affinity with a few of you here. If you go there, you will be astonished to see what happens. Although you have never seen them before, the moment you stand in front of them you will feel that they are your very own. This is because you have been together for many, many lives. This is called soul's affinity.

Twin souls are those that share the same type of capacities and have the same type of experiences together. Soul mates are usually complementary to each other and share with each other a variety of experiences, although each one gains from these experiences according to the mould and pattern of the soul's inner awareness, inner attainment of light and inner sense of manifestation on the earth plane.

Question: As I understand it, there are some forms that are not actually the souls of persons but just forms in the astral world. Will you please explain what kind of consciousness the soulless forms from the astral world have?

Sri Chinmoy: Consciousness is all-pervading. Consciousness you have, I have, everybody has. Consciousness is the light which embodies life itself. Light and life, life and light, comprise consciousness. But in the astral body the life that consciousness has does not operate or take part in the physical world. When consciousness is functioning in a particular plane, it has to adjust itself to that particular plane. The consciousness that we feel or see in the astral plane is not very satisfactory when we want to fulfil the necessary demands of the outer world.

Question: Is there as much reality in astral travelling as in meditation?

Sri Chinmoy: Meditation, if it is real meditation, transcends all astral travelling. Real meditation means conscious oneness with the Absolute. When we have conscious oneness with the Absolute, we do not have to travel anywhere, because the Omnipresent and Omniscient are within us. The highest meditation will offer us the Omnipresence of God. And while we are in His Omnipresence, there is no necessity for astral travelling, for the entire universe is within us. That is what meditation can and does give us.

Question: Have you heard of a kind of spiritual psychology where people try to bring out the supposedly negative aspects and get rid of them, resulting in finally what they call the 'clear' person, who is rid of all personal defects.

Sri Chinmoy: We always say that it is necessary to empty oneself. If you have a vessel which is not filled with the highest consciousness, then it has to be emptied. Only then can your highest consciousness enter into the vessel.

Negative thought, undivine qualities in the nature: we are always dealing with these things in our spiritual life. But by constantly dealing with the negative forces, the unlit qualities in us, we cannot run towards the light. If the vessel is filled with dirt, then we have to empty it and fill it with divine things.

The tiny vessel which we have inside us has to be kept purified and empty so that every day we can fill it with light. But if we constantly dig up the dirt without paying attention to filling ourselves with light, what will happen? After digging the vast quantity of dirt that we have in our conscious mind, we will then enter into the field of the subconscious, then into inconscience. Finally, we shall see what we were some three thousand or four thousand years ago: we shall see an animal, or just a tree, or a solid piece of stone. Now what benefit do we get from this? If we want to go to the source of our evil, dark, corrupt ideas and activities, we shall end up at the very source of destruction or imperfection. We have to be very careful about this.

From your explanation of this kind of psychology, I think that spirituality encompasses it. That is to say, if you care for aspiration, what has to be rejected will automatically be rejected and whatever has to be transformed will be transformed.

Question (about the month of September, 1972, which was a period of great turmoil in the inner world): Wouldn't it be easier on you if some of the things that are happening in the inner world were manifested on the outer plane, instead of your having to take them all on yourself in the inner world?

Sri Chinmoy: No, it would be worse. If they were manifested on earth it would be very frightening, very frightening. This death force is hovering around us like anything. It is just snatching. Whom will it snatch next? It is like a mad elephant. A mad elephant moves around indiscriminately. It does not know where to trample and whom to kill. The forces of this month of September are like that. They are very bad.

I am so happy that in the month of September [1972] we have not lost anybody. This month has been really the worst month. Sometimes I literally cry when I walk along the street. I say, "O God, why have You created this particular month?"

Question: Why did He, Guru?

Sri Chinmoy: It was decided many, many years ago. Hundreds of years ago this was done.

Question: Can the death forces take anyone at any time, even if it is not in their destiny to die just then?

Sri Chinmoy: No, the cosmic law operates. If it is not your time they will not catch you. But this is a special month: September, 1972. This month it is as though the light has gone away; there is a spiritual blackout. When there is a little light, then the dark, hostile forces are afraid of doing things, for fear of being caught. But when there is total darkness, then the mischievous fellows can do anything they want. This particular month of September is like that. Everything is dark, so anything they want to do they can do.

Explanatory Notes

*The explanatory notes were selected from
Sri Chinmoy's writings, up to and including 'Yoga'.
Entries thereafter are by the editor.*

Aspiration
Aspiration is our soul's mounting cry to reach the Highest and to bring down the Highest into the earth's consciousness.

Chakras
There are three principal channels through which this life-energy flows. These channels meet together at six different places. Each meeting place forms a centre. Each centre is round like a wheel. Indian spiritual philosophy calls these centres *chakras*. All real spiritual Masters, from the very depth of their experience, say that it is better to open the heart centre first and then try to open the other centres.

God-Realisation

God-Realisation is nothing short of a spiritual science which puts an end to suffering, ignorance and death. But we have to realise God for His sake and not for our sake. To seek God for one's own sake is to feed one's ceaseless desires in vain. But to seek God for His sake is to live in His universal consciousness; in other words, to be one with Him absolutely and inseparably.

Guru

A real spiritual Master is one who has attained God-realisation. Everyone is one with God, but the real spiritual Master has established his conscious oneness with God. At any moment he can enter into a higher consciousness and bring down messages from God to those disciples who have faith in him. The Master, if he is genuine, represents God on earth for those seekers who have real aspiration and faith in him. He has been authorised or commissioned by God to help them.

The real Teacher, the real Guru, is God Himself. But on earth He will often operate in and through a spiritual Master. The Master energises the seeker with inspiration and, in the course of time, through the infinite Grace of the Supreme, offers the seeker illumination.

The Guru is not the body. The Guru is the revelation and manifestation of a divine power upon earth.

Supreme

There is one God called by many different names. I like the term 'Supreme'. All religious faiths have the same God but they address Him differently. A man will be called 'father' by one person, 'brother' by another and 'uncle' by another. Similarly, God is also addressed in various ways, according to one's sweetest, most affectionate feeling. Instead of using the word 'God', I use the word 'Supreme' most of the time. When we say 'Supreme', we are speaking of the Supreme Lord who not only reaches the absolute Highest, but all the time goes beyond, beyond, and transcends the beyond.

Third Eye

The Third Eye, also called Ajna chakra, is located between and a little above the eyebrows. It is the most powerful centre. He who has mastery over the Ajna chakra destroys his dark past, hastens the golden future and manifests the present in a supremely fulfilling way.

Vital

Each human being is composed of five elements: body, vital, mind, heart and soul. There are two vitals in us: one is the dynamic vital and the other is the aggressive vital. The vital embodies either divine dynamism or hostile aggression. When the aspirant brings the soul's light to the fore, the hostile aggression changes into the divine dynamism and the divine dynamism is transformed into the all-fulfilling supreme reality.

Emotion and the vital are two different things. You can say that the vital is the house and in that house emotion is the tenant. The most predominant emotion is the vital emotion. But emotion can also be in the body, in the mind and in the heart.

Yoga

Yoga means union, conscious union with God. We are one with the Self, but we are not now aware of it. We can become aware of it only when we consciously practise spirituality; and for that we need aspiration. When we are marching along the path of aspiration, our soul will automatically blend with our physical being and the physical being will devotedly listen to the dictates of the soul. Then we will see that our inner life and our outer life have become totally one.

Yoga is neither a philosophy nor a religion. Yoga transcends both philosophy and religion; at the same time, it houses both religion and philosophy. Religion and philosophy can lead a human being up to God's palace, while Yoga means union with God, man's conscious union with God.

Peter Hurkos (1911-1988)

Peter Hurkos was an acclaimed psychic. Born in Dordrecht, Holland, he acquired his psychic gift in 1941 after falling from a ladder and suffering a brain injury. Upon regaining consciousness, he discovered he had developed an ability to pierce the barriers that separate the past, present and future and gained worldwide acceptance as a psychic detective.

Sri Ramakrishna (1836-1886)

Sri Ramakrishna was a great Indian spiritual Master whose life was a testament to truth, universality, love and purity. When he as a young man became a temple priest, he was seized by an unquenchable thirst for union with God, and he immersed himself in intense meditation and other spiritual practices.

Ramakrishna was constantly absorbed in the thought of God. He would often go into high spiritual states where he would merge with the Infinite Reality. For him, the Vedantic teaching of unity of all existence was more than theory; he literally saw, and knew, this to be true.

In his thirst for the divine, Ramakrishna followed different religious paths including various branches of Hinduism. Not content to stop there, however, he also practiced Islam and later meditated deeply on Christ, experiencing the same divine Reality through these non-Hindu paths. Thus, he came to the conclusion, based on his direct experience, that all religions lead to the same goal.

Swami Vivekananda (1863-1902)

Swami Vivekananda was the most notable disciple of Sri Ramakrishna, who demonstrated the essential unity of all religions. Vivekananda's inspiring personality was well known both in India and in America during the last decade of the nineteenth century and the first decade of the twentieth. The unknown monk of India suddenly leapt to fame at the Parliament of Religions held in Chicago in 1893, at which he represented Hinduism. His vast knowledge of Eastern and Western culture, as well as his deep spiritual insight, fervent eloquence, brilliant conversation, broad human sympathy and colourful personality, gave him an almost irresistible appeal to the many Westerners with whom he came into contact.

About the Author

Sri Chinmoy was born in the village of Shakpura in East Bengal, India (now Bangladesh) in 1931. He was the youngest of seven children in a devout family. In 1944, after the passing of both of his parents, he joined his brothers and sisters at the Sri Aurobindo Ashram, a spiritual community near Pondicherry in South India. He meditated for several hours a day, having many deep inner experiences. It was here that he first began writing poetry to convey his widening mystical vision. He also took an active part in Ashram life and was a champion athlete for many years.

Heeding an inner command, Sri Chinmoy moved to the United States in 1964 to be of service to spiritual aspirants in the Western world. During the 43 years that he lived in the West he opened more than 100 meditation Centres worldwide and served as spiritual guide to thousands of students. Sri Chinmoy's boundless creativity found expression not only in poetry and other forms of literature, but also in musical composition and performance, art and sport. In each sphere he sought to convey the diverse experiences that comprise the spiritual journey: the search for truth and beauty, the struggle to transcend limitations, and the supremely fulfilling communion of the human soul with the Divine.

As a self-described student of peace who combined Eastern spirituality and Western dynamism in a remarkable way, Sri Chinmoy garnered international renown. In 1970 at the request of U Thant, the third Secretary-General of the United Nations, he began the twice-weekly peace meditations for delegates and staff members at UN headquarters that continued until the end of his life. Sri Chinmoy enjoyed a special friendship with many international luminaries including President Mikhail Gorbachev, Mother Teresa, President Nelson Mandela and Archbishop Desmond Tutu.

On 11 October 2007, Sri Chinmoy passed behind the curtain of Eternity. His creative, peace-loving

About The Author

and humanitarian endeavours are carried on worldwide by his students, who practise meditation and strive to serve the world in accordance with his timeless teachings.

For more information about Sri Chinmoy kindly visit www.srichinmoy.org

Learn to meditate with the Sri Chinmoy Centre

Sri Chinmoy Centres give meditation classes in over 350 cities all over the world. Sri Chinmoy asked his students to offer these classes to the general public free of charge, as he felt that the inner peace that meditation could bring was the birthright of each individual.

Find a meditation class near you on www.srichinmoycentre.org

Recommended Books by Sri Chinmoy

Seeking Perfect Health
Spiritual Secrets to Staying Healthy

This comprehensive book addresses the spiritual secrets of health by considering the connection between mind and body, health and karma, how to receive life energy from healthy diet and sleep, dealing with stress and depression, exercises for losing weight and overcoming insomnia, why a healthy body is important for spiritual practice and many other relevant topics.

(www.bluebeyondbooks.co.uk)

The Adventure of Life
On Yoga, Meditation, and the Art of Living

A modern-day spiritual manual that encourages the reader to embrace new ideas, adding a deeper, spiritual dimension to one's life. In a clear and accessible way, Sri Chinmoy speaks about the spiritual art of living, society and religion, as well as popular topics such as chakras, occult powers and the end of the world. He also introduces us to a modern spiritual lifestyle with focus on health, diet, sport, family life and the workplace.

(www.lifeadventure.net)

222 Meditation Techniques

These 222 guided exercises, the largest collection of meditation techniques in one book, are suitable for both beginners and advanced seekers who wish to explore the world of meditation. From breathing exercises, guided meditations and the use of mantras, to special exercises for runners, artists and musicians, ways to overcome depression, stress and bad habits, and even losing weight, this book offers a truly broad canvas of possibilities.

(www.themeditationbook.net)

Sport & Meditation

The Inner Dimension of Sport

This is a unique book, which challenges our preconceptions of our physical capacities and of the limitations of age. It includes specific exercises concerning meditation, concentration and mantra as aids to the focus needed in all forms of exercise and training. It is this new facet that enables us to achieve peak performance, to get more from exercise and to enjoy robust and lasting health and wellbeing.

World champions such as Carl Lewis, Tatyana Lebedeva, Tegla Loroupe, Bill Pearl and Paul Tergat share their own inner secrets and spiritual perspectives on training and competition in anecdotes peppered throughout the book.

(www.sportandmeditation.com)

Angels and Fairies

In this beautifully illustrated book Sri Chinmoy offers profound insight into the connection between angels and fairies and the role that these beings play in relation to us, with the confidence of someone who has attained free access to the inner realms.

(www.bluebeyondbooks.co.uk)

Heart-Wisdom-Drops

Inspiring Aphorisms for Every Day

This collection of 55 inspirational cards makes an excellent gift. Each card features an aphorism and meditative painting by Sri Chinmoy. For those seeking hope, peace of mind and life-wisdom these cards offer inspiration, and are a guide to a happy, harmonious and spiritually grounded daily life.

(www.wisdom-cards.com)

For more books kindly visit www.bluebeyondbooks.co.uk